TURNING AROUND A TROUBLED SCHOOL

A journey of school renewal

PETER HUTTON

Practical, personal and insightful! Everyone who cares about education should read this book.

Professor Pasi Sahlberg
Professor of Education Policy at the University of New South Wales

I have written several times about Templestowe College, or TC as it has become known, as an excellent example of a school that makes the personalisation of learning possible! I have visited the school multiple times, talked with the students and teachers, and of course had numerous wonderful conversations with the former principal and author of this book, Peter Hutton.

The school is truly amazing and a great example of how a school can create an environment for students to take control and to be their own leaders. Thankfully, Peter Hutton has written this book, which gives an exceptional account of the beginning of the innovation and transformation journey at TC. I have great confidence that this book will be an inspiration and provide an irresistible challenge for all school leaders interested in educational transformation.

Professor Yong Zhao
New Foundation Professor at the University of Kansas

I have no doubt this will be influential with schools. Many principals live in a world where following the rules has led them to success, or where they exist in a 'matrix' where they can't see beyond. This book will provide liberation to experiment, make mistakes and challenge. It is full of the most practical, helpful and illuminating ideas about all aspects of leading a school from the operational to the more visionary.

Dr Alex Stol
Friend and expert in Adaptive Cultures

DEDICATIONS

I dedicate this book to the influence and memory of Sir Ken Robinson. Through his now-famous TED talks, he showed clearly that the current schooling system does not serve many of our most creative, unique and vulnerable young people and may even damage them. I had the great pleasure of meeting Sir Ken on a number of occasions and even co-presented with him on a panel in Melbourne. In spite of our plans, he never did make it to visit Templestowe College but was always interested and encouraging about what we were doing. His early death impacted me. The challenge that I would put to the reader is to manifest Sir Ken's ideas to the extent you can within your current role. Only action will make a difference.

A special mention to my dear colleague, TC Deputy Principal Sally Holloway, who was with me on the journey from day one to day three thousand! In one of our first meetings we were talking about what quality defined each of us. You said "Loyalty", and you never let me down.

I would also like to acknowledge the support and encouragement that I have received over the years from my family. To my parents Heather and Jim, for not holding me back with my wild ideas – from my door-to-door peep hole installation business at twelve to allowing me to mortgage the family home to fund the rise (and subsequent fall) of my property development business at nineteen. I am not sure what you were thinking, but I always felt you had faith in me.

To the three powerful women in my life. Fiona, my wife of twenty-six years and partner in business and in life, it is not always easy living with someone who regularly wakes you at 4am saying, 'I have an idea!' Thank you for being my rock, advisor and often translator for my ideas into a form that is more easily understood and accepted. To our daughters, Zoe and Jemima, who I love more than life itself, both of whom are currently making a difference in the world via a medical pathway – we look on with delight as to how you will contribute positively to the world.

CONTENTS

INTRODUCTION

A TRANSFORMATIONAL JOURNEY

I am about to give birth. Obviously not to a child as my sex precludes me as does my age, but instead to something living that has grown inside me over the last few years. A long gestation, I grant you, and I have increasingly waddled around with it, felt it grow, contemplated its future, worried over it, and known the inevitability that it would one day have to be born or it would atrophy and die inside of me. The loss and grief I would feel would be significant, as though a part of me had died too, never growing to reach its potential, and take its part in the world however humble that role might be. I have always struggled with patience – I tend to be a starter but not a natural finisher. I have tried to rush this labour, felt the contractions and started to push the process forward, but it was not the right time. I now sit in my bed, computer on my lap. I know it is time. The delivery will not be quick, at times it will be painful and at times raw. Once the writing process begins in earnest, I know my birthing plan will inevitably need to be discarded, and what will be will be. It has started and although this is a very private and intimate experience, I invite you to join me for this journey.

I have endeavoured to convey the raw human story of one school's transformation and renewal as well as my inner journey over this time. If this were just a history of the change journey at Templestowe College, this might be of interest to perhaps a few hundred people. My intent is somewhat bigger and more audacious. The aim is to use my journey as a school leader and the school of which I was part of at that time, as the foundational characters in a story of transformation at the cutting edge of school innovation. It is my hope to inspire and guide other school leaders in how they might explore their own potential for serving their communities more fully, and ultimately through the collective impact of these new more 'aware' leaders, accelerate the transformation of schooling as we currently know it.

WHAT IS YOUR AIM?

When you think about the word 'transformation' in any context, it can seem like a dauntingly huge and unattainable goal. Transform comes from two Latin words, 'trans' meaning to *move* across or beyond and 'formare', to form. So, transformation is a (generally positive) change process towards a new state. Something that has been transformed has a new look (external), feel (internal) or purpose (function), but anything *moving towards* this new different state is in a process of transformation.

If you set 'educational transformation' as your goal, that is a wildly scary and ambitious aim indeed, as education encompasses all aspects of the process of learning. A subset of that is the 'transformation of schooling', which still feels quite unattainable. Where are we talking? Globally, nationally, our school system, our district? Imposter syndrome will soon break out. Who are YOU to change the system?

But if you are a school leader, having the goal to 'transform your school', to positively and significantly change the way it looks and operates, how it feels in terms of how people experience the environment and how people relate to one another, or the purpose, the reason for existence, the mission and vision that guides people in doing what they do, seems suitably aspirational, but distinctly more achievable.

Take-aways:

- Transformation is a process, not an end point
- Transformation requires there to have been a change in the look, feel or purpose
- Transformation requires *action* to have been taken to achieve this change.

It is my hope that this book will support you to be a transformational school leader.

I have tried to write as honestly as I can so that leaders, both current and emerging, can get an inside view of what it feels like to be going through a very public leadership challenge. We read much about school leadership, but often not how it genuinely feels to be in the hot seat through tough times of school transformation. I hope that there is some value in this for you. For me, it has at the least been cathartic.

I invite you to play with the ideas presented here, sit with them, test them out in your own context, consider what resonates and what doesn't. I am all for research-informed innovation, but don't intellectualise this too much until you are at the point of planning any rapid build-outs. If you look to the research in the first instance, for your inspiration, you will find only numbers and ideas of those things already previously explored by other 'doers' and in contexts that are inevitably different from yours. This is a learning of mine. *Feel* your way through innovation and lead others through it. Use data to inform and confirm or deny assumptions, but don't be led by it. Schools are groups of people interacting together in an ecosystem, not buildings, not tradition, not a mechanical system. If you want evidence of that, walk the halls, sit in a classroom at night or on the holidays. The physical school is simply the husk of what was, when those spaces were filled with living beings.

I am not an academic, I am an intuitive doer. I make things happen. This book is not written from a theoretical or even a research-based point of view. It is the exploration of what worked and what didn't for the school community in Melbourne, Australia, that I led over an eight-year period and what is now adding value to other schools implementing aspects of this style of learning. Hopefully it will add value for you, too. There is a LOT of research available to support why the *Take Control* model of learning works, but in a way, presenting it feels like an effort in self-justification. I am NOT anti-research, quite the contrary, I e-read through audio books and assisted technology, widely and voraciously. I just feel that there is often a gap between the theory and how to make it work. In hindsight, it is the humanity. The human story behind the numbers. Good leaders are well read, informed and listen to the advice of experts. But research is a thirst that can never be quenched. There will always be one more paper, one more TED talk, one more innovative school to visit, one more course to do… (preferably at Harvard), one more speaker to listen to. Are you here now, looking for one more expert's opinion? Have you been on the edu-tourism bus, visiting many other school sites, stalking innovative schools on the web and reading countless articles on LinkedIn? Such experiences are important preparations, and planning and research is a necessary *part* of most successful journeys, but it is only when you make a start to innovate yourself, *to do something*, that you have left the safety of home. Rather than motivate and empower you to act, researching can convince you that you are not yet ready, increase your concern that you may get it wrong and magnify that inner voice 'who are you to change the face of schooling?' Researching, especially undertaking a PhD, can be an excuse for inaction that can take you out of the real game for years. If you are reasonably well informed of research-based practice and have some ideas based on that knowledge that you think would work for your community, then you are ready. Box up all those old books, stop spending your weekend mornings in bed Googling the exploits of others and instead, as you read this book, make a plan and carry it out.

A face marred by dust and sweat and blood

'It is not the critic who counts; not the man who points out how the strong man stumbles, or where the doer of deeds could have done them better. The credit belongs to the man who is actually in the arena, whose face is marred by dust and sweat and blood; who strives valiantly; who errs, who comes short again and again, because there is no effort without error and shortcoming; but who does actually strive to do the deeds; who knows great enthusiasms, the great devotions; who spends himself in a worthy cause; who at the best knows in the end the triumph of high achievement, and who at the worst, if he fails, at least fails while daring greatly, so that his place shall never be with those cold and timid souls who neither know victory nor defeat.'

– Theodore Roosevelt

NB: Please excuse the overt masculinity of this imagery. Consider its time of writing and adapt its meaning to now. This passage certainly helped me keep my nerve at various critical points in those early years.

The Templestowe College (TC) story unfolded at a particular time in a specific context in Victoria, Australia. A proportion of TC's success can be attributed to good fortune and timing. If it had not worked, it is unlikely that you would be reading about our story. It is perhaps noteworthy that unlike many of the most innovative schooling models found around the globe, it occurred within the constraints of a state education system rather than within a less rigid independent school framework. The school community was quite broken, and research shows us that when any organisation is on its knees this can be a factor that triggers radical innovation. However, the enormous value of what has been learnt about student empowered learning through the process should not be dismissed simply because we had a favourable set of conditions. We have since implemented aspects of a *Take Control* model of learning in other diverse settings and the positive impacts have been borne out in remarkably similar ways. I would like to say I had a grand plan and was just pulling the right levers along the way, but my aim in the first two years of my time as principal was the school's survival… pure and simple. I certainly had ideas and values, but at the time, if I could have swapped these for a well-functioning conventional school I would have jumped at the opportunity. I only became a true convert to student empowered learning when I saw the benefits start to play out in front of me.

This is the first of four planned short books, the first three covering three reasonably distinct stages of TC's transformational journey. The final book will explain what a school of the future could look like based on the learnings of TC and all the ideas I have seen implemented by dynamic and impressive educators and their school communities from around the globe and all that I have imagined over my career. The series is intended to move to action anyone who for whatever reason is dissatisfied with the current inflexible educational system as they are experiencing it. You may be a student or parent feeling frustration at the current schooling system and keen to know if there is another way, and if so, good for you wanting some behind-the-scenes information about how to achieve a grassroots change in schools. More likely you are a teacher, departmental leader, school leader, system leader or in my wildest dreams, an Education Minister. Note that it is not the value of the person that I differentiate between, but rather the power that position offers each of us to have a potentially positive influence over the greatest number of people.

This first book is a personal introduction and account of those early survival years. Hopefully it may provide encouragement for anyone undertaking a similar school rescue journey. I hope it provides you with some insight into how to take those initial steps in moving forward, gives you some encouragement that you don't need a hugely well-documented plan or to have all the answers in advance – you just need to start, take some risks, be prepared to admit when things are not working, readjust and move forward.

For those coming from a school environment that is more established and even doing well by conventional measures, I hope it is informative, sets the scene for a broader exploration around innovation and gives you some context about the environment I was operating in.

DISCLAIMER

It must be pointed out that credit for any positive outcomes at either TC or any other school I have interacted with must also rest with those who shared the hard work of planning and implementation. I hold my mental construction of how schools could work, but the success or failure of any initiative is very much in the hands of the participants, the students, parents, educators and leaders. While writing I have reflected on how those who shared the journey will relate and react to what I have written. I imagine that they may get some new insights on what was going on 'behind the scenes'. I also hope that I have been accurate in my portrayal. I even considered calling it a piece of historical fiction to relieve the tension of honesty. In my mind I have had to try and undo and analyse some of the TC marketing messages which I have refined and repeated on thousands of occasions, so much so that even I started to believe it, rather than the actual reality. In writing these books I have looked through photos, read principal articles I had written for the College Council, newsletters and end of year magazines to ensure I have the correct timeline and to try and recapture snippets of my feelings and thoughts from these times. I hope that sharing my inner journey through this process may strengthen others as they realise I really had little idea what I was doing at the time, and was essentially fumbling and intuiting my way through a very, very complex process. It may strengthen and reassure the potential school innovator that you don't need, indeed are unlikely, to have all the answers when you start a journey of transformation in your school.

In writing this book I have a slight fear or premonition that I may come across as arrogant. This is an insecurity and jibe that I have lived with, or *perceived* was being said behind my back, for much of my life. I believe that it comes from having opinions that are outside the norm and yet having the 'audacity' to express them anyway. Well, I am fifty-four, I am over it as most people over fifty are. I will tell it as I see it. Hopefully, this fits in nicely with where the world is headed in terms of authenticity, rawness, transparency and vulnerability. I will endeavour to keep myself intellectually honest and not to make this a processed white loaf. I am me, I have learnt to live with that, I hope you can too.

I invite and welcome you to join with me through the initial survival stage of this journey, the first two years in what would eventually become an eight-year transformation into a school recognised internationally for innovation and empowerment.

Chapter One

MY EDUCATIONAL STORY

EARLY INFLUENCES

As we will be spending some time together, you may wish to know a little about me. When I shared the first draft of this book with family and close friends, they suggested I needed to include more of my background which I was somewhat reluctant to do. 'Who would really care?' was my thought. Bill, my daughter's partner, explained in his very rational way that it might help to explain my thinking and personal biases, which I liked in terms of being transparent. My dearest wife Fiona said that women in particular often want to know the human side behind the story, so I have now added in additional details that may help build a fuller picture.

I am dyslexic. It is not my only defining feature, but it is significant in that I inherently see the world a little differently to most neurotypical people. Growing up in a literacy-based world will do that to a person and tends to teach you that if you follow the rules you will fail. You learn to challenge, bend, disregard, break rules and then apologise. I have read few books other than audio based and as such it seems a little ironic that I should write one, but I feel that I have a message and that it is time to share these thoughts. Out of respect for my fellow dyslexics, I will try to ensure that the audio book is brought out at the same time as any print version.

I grew up in Clayton, Victoria, Australia which was then, and still is, one of the most multicultural areas in the world. At the time housing was relatively cheap, and it was the home of Monash University, one of the new breed of universities of the 1970s that seemed to be based more around learning and equity and less about tradition and conservatism. I recall enjoying my pre-school days playing with the Greek neighbours' baby goat one day and eating it in yiros a few days later. As one of only two white Australian families in the whole street, I was sometimes called Skip after the famous television series, *Skippy*, the bush kangaroo. I grew up with no fear of people from different nationalities and accepted that people were just different, but all basically nice when you got to know them. My days outside the classroom at the local state primary school were filled with friends, fights, smoking, tests of physical strength on the monkey bars, kiss-chasey and lots of playing 'wars'.

Inside the classroom was a less positive story. I was one of the last to get both my pencil licence and pen licence, which I am convinced was given to me by the teacher out of sympathy along with the two students who had clear and significant learning difficulties still labouring through the work tasks using our despised, thick and dust-encrusted crayons. In spite of knowing that I was intelligent in a range of ways, not the least of which were street smarts, my humiliation at the hands of the education system had begun. In Grade 2, I realised that for some reason I just could not get a handle on the concept of spelling and reading out loud as quickly as other kids, I focused more on maths and sport. I was always pretty good at making others laugh and could deflect most attempts at being forced to read out loud to the class by punctuating each sentence with a smart-alec remark until the teacher lost patience and smacked me as you could in those days, sent me out of the room or simply moved on. I found that if you consistently collected the answer cards to the wax-coated self-paced comprehension cards one level ahead of the ones you were supposed to be working on, you could make great progress without detection. 'A minus' was my usual reading grade, performing well using my 'supported method of testing' but I received a repeated comment that I should 'read more for pleasure.' I wish to track down Mrs Demontoni and invite her to gargle broken glass for pleasure. For most dyslexics, reading is simply not a pleasurable activity, but instead a daily experience of ritual humiliation.

With my supportive and doting mother working in clerical administration and boilermaker/welder/taxi owner-driver father, I did not really know what happened at a university other than it was a place where 'smart people went to study'. My uncle and aunty were both schoolteachers and the only people I knew personally who had been to a university. As an only child of working parents, I sometimes stayed with my aunty and uncle on holidays and they seemed the ultimate in sophistication and were positively revered by the wider family. I felt that they really took me under their wing in both an academic development and personal sense, and it seemed like they treated me as a young equal.

My Latvian-Malaysian friend Victor, whose parents were both university-educated, and I would ride our bikes around the university, fishing aluminium cans out of the bins and selling them to the Alcoa-cash-a can-centre for one cent a can. We collected many thousands of cans, but strangely I can never remember cashing them in. I think I became very comfortable with the formidable size of the campus where I would eventually complete a Bachelor of Economics (Accounting), Diploma of Education and Masters of Educational Leadership.

Not really having a knowledge of what to do about secondary education and with a strong rumour circulating that a Year 7 boy had been attacked at the local high school and 'had his balls cut off' my parents asked a teacher friend where they were sending their son. Such rumours were, I assume exaggerated, but it was an incredibly rough school and was enough to convince me to try an alternative. Hence, I ended up travelling by bus an hour each day in very much a *Lord of the Flies* type environment to a large single sex independent school where the kids that did not come from family money attended. The violence and intimidation both on the bus and in every aspect of school life was an almost continual adrenalin rush where my emotions oscillated quickly between fight or flight.

My secondary experience was not an easy time or one that I recall with fondness. I was physically abused by staff as were we all, as part of the school system of official and unofficial sanctions. Through a mixture of hard work and cheating, which also seemed rampant in the school at the time, I managed to get through the six years with reasonable grades. Even though I was struggling with spelling in English, I took two languages as my electives in Year 9, as I was told by friends that otherwise I would be 'left behind with the dumb kids'. I genuinely thank and apologise to those students who both voluntarily and involuntarily helped me get through two years of French and German. There was the odd compassionate and inspiring teacher which all the students delighted in, but most presented as aloof, dispassionate, self-centred and scary. The Principal at the time was an imposing God-like figure with a booming voice whose plan for the boys, which he explained to me some years later, was to 'make them so tough that the best of them could rise within any environment'. I never really asked him what the plan was for the other 80% of students, but the mantra was a clear 'win at any cost' and that victors are the only ones that count.

It is almost thirty-five years since I left the formal schooling system as a student, but many of my beliefs, values and reactions against traditional schooling are rooted in my experiences from that time. I can imagine some of the students who I attended school with saying 'that isn't true, it wasn't that bad, you ended up as a prefect and a captain of various sports', but this IS my recollection, and my feelings are most certainly the memories I hold. My secondary schooling did teach me to be hard, at times to emotionally detach, to repel bullies by sometimes even becoming a bully and that you are the sum of your achievements. It took me a long time to work through and overcome the legacy of these experiences.

What was your school experience as a student?

What was your school experience as a student, and how might this be impacting on your view of schooling now that you are on the other side? Are you rescuing the younger you, perhaps replicating the positive aspect of your own experience for others, or perhaps dealing with some unfinished business? Even though many of us may have already spent many more years in schools as an educator, our own schooling experience has still left a significant impression that can strongly influence the direction of our whole career.

AN IRONIC TEACHER OF EMPOWERMENT – THE AUSTRALIAN ARMY (MY FIRST EXPOSURE TO STUDENT EMPOWERMENT)

I have long had a faith and belief in what young people can achieve. I can trace this confidence in the power of youth back to my first experiences working with the Australian Army Cadet Corps. As an eighteen-year-old, I had been swayed by a TV commercial which showed the exciting life of an Army Reservist, and soon after enlistment found myself on the Officer Training program within the

Australian Army Reserve. After a few years, our course instructor suggested that a number of us should consider volunteering our services at 31 Regional Cadet Unit comprising young people from the ages of thirteen to eighteen. The idea was that we could provide additional military knowledge to these young people and we could simultaneously develop our leadership skills. Turning up on that first night, I was met by a confident young cadet who introduced himself and then took me to the Unit Headquarters which comprised both adult instructors and cadets around the ages of fifteen to eighteen wearing various badges of rank with which I was familiar. I quickly realised that this was not a program being 'done to students' by adult instructors, but rather a youth-run leadership and development organisation, run by young people for young people under a structured military framework.

This was the start of many years of association with Army Cadets, that for a while paralleled my journey as a commissioned Officer in the Army Reserve, until the opportunity for promotion within my first school, Beaconhills College, made me choose between the two careers. My Headmaster, Rick Tudor, a legend in Australian education and himself an ex-Reserve Officer said that I had the potential to become a good Army Officer or good educational leader, but not both at the same time. With the first Iraq War in play and with an inner quandary over why Australia had chosen to become involved in this conflict, I chose to leave the Army and commit myself to education.

Having endured and survived my first year of teaching, with no curriculum resources provided to me and zero supervision as was generally the case in those days, where graduates were expected to sink or swim, I was looking for a leadership challenge. A tactic I learnt early on in my career was if there is no leadership position on offer, create your own and then fill it. I approached Rick and asked him if we could start the Beaconhills School Cadet Unit. Having worked in previous prestigious independent schools with Cadet Units and with his own Army Reservist background, Rick gave the green light. I promised him at least one significant fracture or medical emergency each year, as I did not want the odd training mishap to close down the unit prematurely. Fortunately, after four years of operation we had only experienced one potentially serious injury.

Make your own leadership opportunities

This is an approach I encourage all aspirant leaders to consider. Don't wait to be offered a leadership opportunity, and don't wait for a leadership position to be advertised where you will rightly be in open competition with a range of others, many of whom may be more experienced than you. Spot an opportunity, write a proposal including costings and benefits and put your proposal to the leadership team. On the whole, the world rewards initiative.

What problem can you see in your context that needs fixing? If it is a significant problem, could you come up with a partial solution that you could attempt that would at least improve the situation?

Encouraged by the capacity that I had seen for young people to show genuine leadership for others, one night a week I would teach the prescribed lessons to the student leaders who had volunteered to help start the cadet unit and had received instant promotion to the rank of corporal. The next night they would teach the same lesson to the equally new but younger cadets. The Australian Army has a quite prescriptive format for direct instruction that is scarily reminiscent of John Hattie's High Impact Teaching Strategies. It was easy for young people to follow, prescriptive and reasonably effective:

- 'This lesson is...'
- 'The reason you are taught this is...' (rationale for learning)

- 'By the end of the lesson you will be able to...' (learning objective)
- 'You do it like this... Now do that.' (explicit instruction).

At the same time a few Reservist friends lent support, teaching our 'instant leaders' about the culture and norms of Army leadership. Over time we built a unit with deeply personal relationships among cadets based on trust, respect and loyalty. Looking back, it was quite a wild time in education and the risk levels of the training activities that we were able to conduct back then – including running our own rock-climbing activities, survival courses, river crossings at night and regular escape and evasion activities – would land an educator in prime position on *Today Tonight* if they were done today. Sadly in some ways, but understandably, cadets has gone the way of most organisations and become highly risk-averse. The full impact of a cotton wool upbringing (provided by well-meaning parents) on the mental wellbeing of young people will not be known for some decades, but the significant spike in youth anxiety and depression could be the starting signs.

Young people are capable of far more than we imagine!
ENOUGH!
The school system seeks to control them,
Mould them,
Grade them,
Disempower them.
All that we do reinforces their place in the pecking order.
They must wait their turn,
They are not powerful, and
They cannot be trusted.
We imply that their dreams are unrealistic, naïve, childish, and
Lie that there is no other way, other than through it, and endure it.

– Peter Hutton

During this time with cadets, I saw young people display planning and organisational skills beyond those possessed by most adults. I observed young people at the age of sixteen plan week-long activities with twenty-four-hour-per-day training packages, manage the travel, food, equipment as well as obtaining parental and school permissions. I saw young junior leaders of fourteen resolve disputes within their sections, deal with homesickness, and deliver training at a standard that I had wished my own soldiers had been able to display when I worked with the regular army. For me, the tragedy was returning to school and seeing the same young people that had led with such purpose and confidence reduced by the system to being passive recipients of information, sitting bored in classrooms. I knew I was on to something here. Over the next few years, as the brilliant adult cadet staff worked to develop finer and finer grade skills in these young people, I started to ask myself, 'What if a whole school was run like this?' I had seen movies about military schools in America. Could such a thing be done in Australia, perhaps without the military overlay?

I had become somewhat disenchanted, not with the military itself but the concept that some of the young people I had worked with in cadets were now overseas fighting in battles of questionable legitimacy. Even after two decades, the bonds that were formed among the people who comprised this student-led learning community are very strong. In spite of only seeing each other at the odd reunion or on Facebook, this time remains very special to us all and was monumental in developing my ideas around the usually untapped capacity of young people. After four years the Unit had grown to over ninety cadets, with a dramatically over-representative flow on to formal student leadership positions in the school and I am pleased to report that the Cadet Unit still continues to develop young leaders to this day, recently celebrating its twenty-fifth birthday.

WHAT IS YOUR EDUCATIONAL STORY?

I encourage you to reflect on your own school experience and how that has, and still is, shaping you as both a person, educator and/or parent. Close your eyes and reflect back through your *feelings* about your experience of school. You might wish to write your reflections down in a notebook or journal. This is not the physical, not the sum of your achievements or failures, but the relationships you had with each of the teachers. Try going through your memory by year level at primary school and then specialist subjects, then work by subjects and school leaders at secondary school. You may have school photos or a year-book that can be helpful to anchor your thoughts. What was your relationship like with them? How did they make you feel? What response, if any, did you have to them? Just let it sit with you. Don't take this as a task to be worked through, explore it as you feel the inclination and strength to do so. To skip over this analysis could be a lost opportunity for reflection and growth as an educator. To what degree can you see these experiences during your formative years continuing to influence the way you now see and do school today?

Now consider your range of peers, the older students, the younger ones, your friends, your enemies and those to whom you were indifferent. Think back to any camps and excursions. Think about taking tests. Think about punishments you endured. Think about the politics that played out in the yard.

How has your own schooling experience influenced your view of education now?

What are your recollections and feelings around homework, sporting events, concerts, and receiving your report card? What about your relationship with your parents or care-giver at this time?

If circumstances permit, you might want to ask your parents about their recollections of your time at school. In my own parents' case, it was difficult coming to terms with the fact that the significant financial sacrifices they had made might not actually have been such a positive investment. Keep in mind that it can take some time to move beyond the superficial but the insight you will develop about why you hold certain values and world views about school that you still retain today may be invaluable.

What were the conversations you had with your inner self at that time? Did you keep a journal?

I am not intentionally trying to get you to unearth painful experiences and feelings. It is the self-protective side of human nature to compartmentalise the pain and remake your memories in more affirming ways. Without wanting to sound like a self-help book, you may want to write a poem, a letter to yourself, try to capture your feelings in a photograph, a metaphor or other medium. You may find that you need to repeat this exploration over a number of sessions, particularly if the emotions are strong. It may be that once stirred up over the next days or weeks, new memories will pop into your mind. While I can imagine some people saying, 'enough with the airy fairy stuff, let's get into the meaty details of educational change', taking the time to thoroughly explore these feelings is important as they are the foundation on which you base your assumptions and paradigms and build your mental model of school.

Adolescence can be a tough time. Sit with your experiences and talk with the very young you. Give them comfort that things turned out okay, and assure them that you hear them and that you are doing what you can to make things better for all young people.

WHY WE DO WHAT WE DO

I am a person who has always admired people who do great things. This is because of my understanding and appreciation of the incredible effort, persistence and dedication required to progress from naturally talented to exceptional performance. In some ways it doesn't matter what the great thing is – a golfer skilled at aim and accuracy to the delight of the crowd, an actor capable of bringing an audience to tears or a magician able to distract onlookers so well they question the actual existence of magic. None of these things really matter. What matters is the exceptional performance, something far, far beyond the capability of the average. When this exceptionality is applied to an entrepreneur who can create something unique from nothing, a climate scientist who can simplify complex data without losing accuracy or an engineer designing increasingly natural artificial limbs it leads me to wonder – what is our role as educators? Why do we do what we do?

As educators we are the nurturers of the next generation. As life has become more complex, parents and the government have increasingly looked to educators in schools to be the experts in child and adolescent development, the unqualified but much relied upon psychologists and counsellors. With the reduced impact of religious organisations, schools have become the builders and keepers of our evolving social morality. Schools have become the new church, or community hub for our society.

Much progress has been made in the recognition of LGBTQ+, gender identification, integration of disabilities and addressing bullying and sexism. Educators have taken on the moral responsibility for educating around fairness, equity and respect for human rights, without any explicit authority or direction given by the states or politicians. The action has been taken by the collective individual efforts of leaders and staff members in schools who have seen the social imperative to act in the best interests of young people and for society. We are the social watchdogs expected to detect, and are now mandated to take action, when a student is behaving in a way that may indicate dysfunction outside school. The sanctity of what happens behind closed doors in the home has been irrevocably broken and thankfully we are now no longer allowed to turn a blind eye.

I often say that schooling has not fundamentally changed in over a hundred years, but in regard to the hidden curriculum of schools, the personal development aspect for young people, it has manifestly changed. There is still much to be done but things have already undeniably changed for the better. Regardless of socio-economic status, many young people are exposed to significantly challenging home lives – we are their safety net, their carer, their advisor, their adult stability and their reassurance. When we make a positive difference, particularly for youth at risk, we change their future.

Many educators are passionate about their areas of interest, academic and personal. They often convey their deep level of engagement and interest to students as their enthusiasm can't help but bubble over. This, of course, positively influences young people, often leading them into areas beyond the narrowness of their own home lives and curriculum. While the traditional role as subject deliverer and promoter is still important, it must alter. The world is becoming smaller and the standard of what is required to be an expert is rising. The chances of a student finding a teacher who uniquely matches their own natural talents and interest within their school is statistically improbable. As a profession we must abandon the title of subject expert unless we *really* are. Even if we were once an expert, are we still on the cutting edge in the field? Today, we still have an obligation to expose students to a wide range of learning experiences so they are aware of opportunities, but we also need to acknowledge there is far greater diversity or specialties than any school alone can expose students to. We need to deeply integrate schools within the far broader community where students who have shown interest or aptitude in a subject area are quickly and seamlessly given access to true experts. We can then adopt the role of facilitator, encourager and co-learner. In a global community we are unlikely to be the subject expert, but we *can be* the learning expert if we are willing to open ourselves to that opportunity and undertake ongoing development work.

Students do not have to be the best in the world to be successful, but they will do better if they find and explore their strengths that also tie in with their interests and passions. Educators have the capacity to be expert learning facilitators, and accelerators that support each young person to discover and develop their unique talents.

So, while we may not be the person on the stage, the person held up for public praise or even the one with a more than comfortable living, *we* are the ones that help others succeed. *We* are the ones behind the success of people making significant contributions in the world. Collectively, we are the ones that influence the tone and morality of society and bring exceptional learning experiences and hope to young people.

Educators are in a unique position to exploit opportunities out there that promote greatness in others and bring those opportunities to the attention of young people. We can adapt the learning to be more flexible, more individualised, more accessible and deeply integrated with the community. This empowers ALL young people so that ALL can succeed.

That's why our work is important. That's why we do what we do.

Chapter Two

THE BEGINNING

THE LONG ROAD TO PRINCIPALSHIP

For two years I had been trying to find a principalship in the eastern suburbs, over an hour away from where I was currently Assistant Principal. Our plan was for me to find a school closer to the Melbourne suburb of Bulleen where my family had moved two years earlier for our two girls' academic and sporting needs. However, attempting to move on promotion from a rural region to the much sought-after and highest academically performing Eastern Region of Victoria was not an easy feat. Even though I felt I had quite a strong record of measurable success in previous and current positions, I had applied for and been rejected for twenty-eight principalship positions. In one particular case I was interviewed twice for a position in a school that was commonly regarded as a school in significant trouble, and yet the selection panel made a non-appointment twice. As I saw it, the panel would actually prefer to have no one in the position rather than have me lead their school. This was quite bruising to my ego. I said to my partner Fiona as I put in my last two applications, 'If I don't get one of these, then I'm out of education.'

The value of persistence

Sometimes you do need to be persistent in applying for leadership positions. You are often unaware of the school's real context, or what politics are involved. Later, once the successful applicant had been named, I would often find out that the person was an internal applicant and that sometimes they had already been acting principal for several years, but according to government regulations the position had to be advertised with the absolute assurance that it would be a 'transparent and fair process.' It is nonsense to believe that a selection panel always makes the best, even the second best, decision. They just make a decision.

Hopefully you can use my example of thoughtfully preparing and submitting thirty applications before experiencing success to retain your self-belief and keep applying. Principalship is one of the most powerful positions to make a genuine difference in the lives of a significant number of young people, and we need the very best people in these roles.

APPLYING FOR THE JOB

As part of my preparation for the interview for the Principalship of Templestowe College (TC) I received the applicant information pack, which included the previous year's data on the school's performance. I was somewhat surprised as I looked through the staff opinion data to see that most of it was in the third and fourth quartile. So according to staff, the school was doing a great job. Supportive leadership was in the seventy-eighth percentile, professional interaction, participative decision-making and goal congruence were all in the high seventieth percentiles and student orientation was in the eightieth relative to other state secondary schools. These were all results that I would have been absolutely delighted with at my previous school. What is going on here? Why are student numbers so low, currently sitting at an enrolment of 450, but on the decline from 950 students over the last eight years?

I then opened the file titled student opinion data and the answer became clear. Teacher effectiveness first percentile, stimulating learning environment first percentile and teacher empathy, second percentile as measured relative to other Year 7-12 Victorian government schools. This was further confirmed by the parent opinion data with school improvement focus, stimulating learning environment, learning focus and general satisfaction all hovering under the fifth percentile. Essentially, based on the opinion of students the school was close to the worst school in the state. It was quite obvious that this was a school that was meeting staff needs to the detriment of student needs.

HOW DID THE SCHOOL END UP IN THIS POSITION?

Templestowe College was founded in 1994 as the amalgamation of Templestowe High, which was regarded as quite a well-performing academic school and Templestowe Technical School, during a period where the government of the day was understandably concerned about technical schools pre-determining the pathways and life outcomes for young people. Although based on noble ideals, closing technical schools is widely considered one of the worst systemic decisions made in Victorian education. In this case the academic high school was absorbed into the technical school and to add another layer of difficulty to a new school already about to cope with combining two quite disparate staff cultures together, they brought the highly academic and capable female high school principal to lead the new school. By all accounts she was subjected to a merciless and disgraceful display of bullying and harassment by the male technical school staff and removed to the safety of the Regional Office. The Department then employed a principal with a reputation as a 'head kicker' to 'sort out the place', but like so many head kickers they kicked almost everyone, the environment became toxic and the 'good' staff left as well as the bad. This period was complicated by the prosecution and jailing of a staff member who had been in a sexual relationship with a student. The public relations fall-out was poorly handled and the school saw a steep drop in enrolments. At that time a gentle and caring principal was appointed to help the school heal, however the situation probably required more decisive and drastic action. The leadership team and council were trying to position the school a little like a private school with strong traditional values and broad programs, but this market was already well and truly taken by other successful state and independent schools and the student results did not support the narrative. For the first few years in the school, I lamented that it was a pity that I had not picked up the job before the school had reached the broken level it had.

Why go into this detail, the personalities of the previous school leaders? Because in taking over the leadership of a school in trouble, the new leader has to firstly understand the forces and circumstances that led to the current cultural state and then to craft a compelling and believable narrative to 'sell' to the community as to why things will now be different. I now understand this to be critical, but frankly was lucky to have stumbled through this transition relatively unscathed at the time. While being conscious to try and not disrespect my three predecessors, two of whom I had met and respected very much as people and educators, I developed a narrative that 'TC's leadership story is like the story of *Goldilocks and the Three Bears*, the first leader was too hard, the second one too soft, but the third is just right!'

Create a compelling new community narrative

Parents considering enrolling into a broken school, or one in significant need of change, need a simple and believable account of how the school got into this state and why it is now going to change. They need this so they can recount the same story to others in the community when they are inevitably asked, 'Why would you possibly consider enrolling your child there?'

IT STARTED WITH A VISION

When I was interviewed for the Principalship there were a number of standard questions, but it was clear that the real criteria were 'Do you have a compelling vision for the school and can you sell it?' We were given twenty minutes to present. It was quite a cathartic process, but knowing this was my last pitch, whether I succeeded or failed, I really thought about the school I wanted to develop and lead. The vision I developed was 'To be a dynamic and caring learning community, recognised for future-focused personalised learning.'

While I am generally sceptical of vision statements, I genuinely believed in this one and started to sell it once I was employed at TC. I use the term 'sell' deliberately. At the time no one really wanted or was even prepared to entertain the notion of coming to TC. Our first task was to try and staunch the flow of students to other schools across all year levels. We had to offer hope, a realistic possibility that things could not only improve, but be better than students and their parents could even imagine.

Drawing on my limited marketing experience from my undergraduate business degree, I wondered, 'What would students like their ideal environment to be like?' A place:

- with freedom to choose what they wanted to learn
- where the work wasn't too hard or too easy

- with a safe environment where they felt respected and cared for
- where *their* dreams were considered valid and treated as potentially attainable
- where learning was fun and not boring
- where students had some choice over who they worked with.

Fortunately, I got the call saying that I had been successful in my application for the Principalship of Templestowe College. After hanging up the phone, I literally danced in my office. After thirty applications for schools located up to an hour away from our home, it happened that Templestowe College was the neighbouring school to where our family had lived for the past two years.

THE TC CREW

A very 'hands on' School Council

My initial research had shown me that the school was in trouble, but at the time I did not really appreciate how seriously. When I met Tracey, the Chair of College Council, I was impressed at how passionate, capable and clearly committed she was to ensure that the school not only survived but started to thrive. She had been a long-time supporter of the school and in many ways she along with the Council had to a larger degree than I have ever seen in a government school, assumed a lot of control over day-to-day decision-making. It certainly went well beyond mere governance. I was, however, slightly disconcerted to find that the Chair had moved her own two children from TC to a neighbouring school. I was not sure this presented to the outside world that she had confidence we could turn this situation around. I was also a little uncertain as to how 'involved' the School Council would want to remain. When I was principal for the briefest of times in an independent school, I had experienced how disastrous an overly involved Board could be, particularly when the school needed such rapid changes. I was assured by Tracey and the other Council members on the panel that while they had been carrying the school for some time, they were very keen to give full control back to the new principal, but they would be there to provide support. True to their word, this was the response and while principal for eight years I enjoyed a very harmonious, supportive and productive relationship with each College Council President and Council.

A loyal deputy

When I was appointed, I asked the selection panel if either of Templestowe College's current two deputies had applied for the principal position. Sally, the senior of the two deputies, had. When we met on the first day of the term three holidays, I raised this matter with her asking how she felt about not having received the job, and that if she wished to apply out for a principalship that I understood and would support her application. Sally said that she had no choice but to have applied. As she expressed in her very pragmatic way, 'What if I hadn't applied and an idiot got the job! I could never have forgiven myself.' It was a little too soon in our relationship to determine if she thought an idiot had been appointed to the role, but Sally voluntarily gave up every weekday of that two-week holiday, working to bring me up to speed on how the school worked and to explore ways that we could start rebuilding. We ended up working together for the duration of my eight-year tenure as Principal. Undoubtedly, Sally became the keeper of the new culture we developed as well as being the driving force in getting change implemented rapidly and efficiently on the ground.

Meeting the staff for the first time

Before officially starting at the school, I had offered all the staff, both teaching and support, the opportunity to come in during the term three school holidays and meet with me, either personally or in small groups. I was unsure of what the take-up rate would be, given it was the holidays. I was very pleased when all except a few individuals who were interstate or overseas during this period and were profusely apologetic, came in and met with me. I asked them to have considered three basic questions. Based on their experience and knowledge of TC, 'What should we stop doing, start doing and keep doing?' As well as identifying a number of specific operational items, the overwhelming message was, 'Do anything, do it quickly and stop asking us.' I later discovered that the department had previously brought in a range of consultants to explore with the staff what was going wrong and that the staff honestly felt that they didn't have the answers internally to fix the situation. I presented the summation of my findings at a full staff meeting and said if this was not the message intended to be communicated to me, down to an individual, then now was the time to disagree. While my preferred leadership style was more along the lines of co-evolved/collaboration, this was the mandate I needed in those first few years, to create a 'benevolent dictatorship.'

I felt that it was important that the staff knew the precarious situation the school was in, but even then I shielded them from the full reality. It really was a balancing act between having them informed and on board and filling them with terror that would inevitably be sensed by existing and prospective parents. I confess to often rounding our new enrolment numbers up to start a positive message that things were improving to circulate through the community. I did have ethical concerns around doing this, but settled with the rather uncomfortable notion that 'the end justifies the means'.

MY FIRST DAY

Of course, I was nervous on my first official day as Principal but also hugely excited. With embarrassment but honesty, I admit to having practised introducing myself many times in the mirror. 'Peter Hutton, Principal, Templestowe College,' aiming for just the right level of self-assurance, friendliness, as well as familiarity and comfort with my new title as I thrust my hand out. Clearly this has become something of a hallmark of my persona, as my teenage children would walk around mocking me, thrusting their hand out for a firm handshake and saying 'Peter Hutton!' then bursting into laughter.

As I parked my Subaru Forester in the Principal's car park, I felt this strange feeling like I was putting on my dad's shoes. Due to an early career break where I was appointed as Deputy of Braemar College, an independent school in Woodend, at the relatively young age of thirty-one, I had been a deputy principal in two roles for ten years. Now at forty-one, it was my chance to be the actual leader of this community. What first impression would I make? Sometimes it's the small details. What would people think of my car? Not too flashy but still nice. I probably should have cleaned it! Did this reveal a lack of attention to detail, or a more casual 'real' approach to life? Not trying too hard to impress, perhaps? As I got out of the car and walked across the driveway, I noticed for the first time the reflective tint on all the windows along the administration building and imagined the eyes of somewhat nervous staff as I approached. A new principal can make a huge difference to a school community and everyone is rightly a little nervous to see what the new incumbent will be like. It almost always changes power balances within the school and this can be unsettling. Just like the new principal, people are usually keen to make a positive impression.

No doubt my hyper-vigilance and self-awareness was far greater than anyone else's but this is how it felt.

Students helped in shaping the environment

It would take a year or two before I and some students and staff took to removing this reflective laminate coating with razor blades and lots of cleaning products to remove the sticky residue during an end-of-year school clean-up. It felt like an act of liberation as we opened up the administration and meeting room to the outside world. It felt like we were symbolically embracing greater transparency and ripping off the tightly adhered film was weirdly satisfying. Having students help with maintenance tasks was a nuance of the TC culture at the time. Students felt that it was their school and would often not even wait to be asked but jump in and help do whatever was being done.

As I reached for the front doors to the school, I saw the most bizarre sign. 'No Students Allowed.' I was taken aback. Why were they not allowed? Presumably as they would then be entering through the foyer? Were they in some way regarded as second-class citizens? Perhaps their behaviour was such that they were likely to make a bad impression on parents waiting in the foyer? Wow, my first test already and I was not in the door yet. Would it be wrong to remove it before asking? Was it my school yet? At what point does this transference of leadership take place? Would it be disrespectful to make an assumption, or was this a call I could now make? What message would it send if I removed it? Certainly the sign was working, because we had no students!

The sign from my first day

In the end I decided that I would remove it. My first decision made. The first step in changing a culture, from students being seen as something to be controlled and 'done to', to people at the centre of our work, and treated with respect.

A BAD START TO STUDENT NUMBERS

When I started as Principal at Templestowe College, initially I wanted to simply establish a functional school. I did not set out with an aim of creating a school known for radical innovation. We just needed to survive the first twelve months.

The school's precipitous decline was well known; there was a genuine fear that the school was going to close, with the School Council told on two separate occasions by the Regional Director that the school was no longer viable. In Australia, it is politically unwise for the government to be seen to be closing schools. Instead, the Education Department will allow a school to continue to operate, sometimes well past the point at which the school is providing an adequate education, and as student numbers decline, wait for the school to be starved of funds until ultimately the School Council must request that the school be closed and everyone put out of their misery. There was also the widely held perception that the Education Department or Treasury were quite keen to sell the sixteen acres of land given that Templestowe is located in one of the more affluent areas of Melbourne.

The position brief for the Principal role had said that the school had approximately 450 students. Knowing that often the selection panels inflate these numbers to make the position seem more appealing, I was not surprised to arrive and find 423 students on the school roll. What I had not counted on was that it was the start of Term 4 and in two weeks, after the VCE exams, we would lose 160 graduates and we had just twenty-three students enrolled for Year 7 the next year. I had arrived thinking I would be building from 450 and within two weeks, had just 263 students rattling around the sixteen-acre campus. Sometimes while on those early tours, prospective families would ask, 'Do you actually have students on campus today?' to which I would respond, 'Well, you are here on a slightly unusual day, all our Year 10s are out on work experience and our Year 9s are on the City Experience program.' The only problem was that they weren't…. the students they could see were all the students we had! While lying is ethically wrong, the desperation faced by principals of struggling schools is very real and I would ask that readers and listeners not judge too harshly unless they have experienced similar stressful situations, and in this case, it was not even a problem of my making.

After my first regional principals' meeting, I was taken out for lunch by the three other local secondary principals. After introductions, welcomes and pleasantries, the topic came around to TC and its viability. It was made clear that they thought I seemed like 'a good bloke', that they wanted to be supportive, but that the school was 'going down' and that it would be best that I was not on it when it did so. One of the principals of a larger school knew that he would resign from his role in the next few months to take up another appointment and his advice was 'get a few quick runs on the board and then get the hell out of there' and apply for his role. I was quite scared by these comments coming from three very experienced principals who knew the local context far better than I did. I explained that while I did not want to be at the helm of a sinking ship, in the few weeks I had already been there, that I had made too many personal commitments to the students, staff and prospective parents that I would be there to see the current group of students graduate, that I could not skip out on them in spite of having only a small chance that we could turn the school around.

When I started at TC, a close friend gave me a thick handmade journal to record the progress of the school's new journey. The cover was handcrafted blue leather and the pages were handmade and bound. It was a beautiful book. It remained untouched in my office cupboard until the day I left. In those early days I thought about journalling in it several times, but I did not want to use such a beautiful book to record the demise of the school, as I lacked that much confidence in the chances of turning the school around. In my eight years at TC, I could never start the journal because the journey always seemed so incomplete and still somewhat precarious. It is only now, with three years of hindsight since leaving the school that the learnings of the journey have become clearer to me and hopefully worthy of relaying. I still have and treasure this journal, its pages still blank and devoid of written words, but for me the anxiety that it invoked at the time, now proven to have been unwarranted, is part of the journey itself. It now awaits my next educational adventure – starting my own school from scratch!

One of my first directions for outreach was to our local primary schools. In talking with my adjoining primary school Principal colleague, Anne, I found that because Templestowe College finished at 3pm and their school finished at 3.30pm, a number of our younger students who had been former students of the primary school with younger siblings still there, were returning after our school day finished and terrorising the younger students and not treating the staff and waiting parents respectfully. This PR nightmare was quickly remedied by moving our finishing time back to finish ten minutes *later* than the primary school and thus giving their students an opportunity to get off site un-accosted. Of course, I ultimately wanted our students' behaviour to change, but that would take time and that was something we didn't have.

'But we have always done it this way'

This situation had existed for years and done immeasurable damage to the school's reputation as well as the misery our students dealt out to younger students. It is amazing to me how many poor processes we retain in schools simply because things have always been done like that.

What issues create, or have the potential to create, a poor public image for your school? How could small modifications turn these situations around?

Anne and I had a positive meeting and I asked if it would be possible to put up a promotional sign on her school's front fence saying that Templestowe College was located at the rear of her school and that we had an exciting new vision. One of the difficulties and peculiarities of the school site was that the entrance was located at the end of what looked like a suburban court and had zero road frontage. I felt this put us at a significant disadvantage as it was out of sight, out of mind, and that as a fellow state school, Anne might support our new endeavours. Her response was polite but unequivocal, 'I genuinely wish you well and want you to succeed, but I want as little tying your school to mine in the minds of our parents as humanly possible.' Ouch! I was a little taken back. We were clearly on our own.

As time went by Anne and the primary school staff ended up offering us many opportunities to present a positive message to their parents, such as inviting us to address their school council, present information sessions to interested parents, acknowledge our presence at the drama and art show, and generally talk up our efforts in the broader school community. For this support when our school was on its knees, I will be forever grateful. Having now supported a number of struggling state schools to reimagine and rebuild themselves, it amazes me how competitive and isolationist many state school leaders are and the lack of support successful schools give to those who struggle within a so-called system. I am perhaps even more frustrated that Regional Directors do not take greater steps to ensure that schools are working more collaboratively to ensure that all state schools function as effective and successful schools.

One of the most demoralising experiences in that first term was walking around the grounds and hearing students talk openly about where they were going next year. One popular student with an intention of moving could easily take a number of follower-friends with them. Where possible I would engage these students in conversation, ask why was it that they were feeling they wanted to leave, where possible assure them that changes would be made and say it was a pity because they would be missing out on... a laptop, a new program of some kind, to choose their own subjects or being given the opportunity to take control of their own education and be treated like an adult. It didn't always work, but it possibly kept a few more in the school than otherwise would have been the case.

WHAT CHANGES DID THE STUDENTS WANT?

When I interviewed the students and asked them the same questions I had earlier asked the staff, 'What should we stop doing, start doing and keep doing?' one of the things they asked for was the introduction of a school blazer. They explained that when students went to the city or visited other schools they tended to feel like 'the povo school', short for poverty-stricken. I did not want the students to feel this way and so in the spirit of 'if the students want it they will get it', a student design committee was formed and the students got blazers. Later on, I was also more than a little happy that we had taken this direction at the request of students, because if we were going to do some out-there, radical educational things then we might need to become chameleons. I envisaged parents saying, 'Well how radical can they be? They introduced a blazer, didn't they!'

Chapter Three

AN AUDIT OF THE SCHOOL'S STRENGTHS

QUESTIONING AND LISTENING

When any new principal starts at an existing school, they are advised to ask lots of questions but even more importantly to listen… a lot. This is very good advice for the whole of your tenure. It is quite foolhardy to come in and start making decisions before you have a clear understanding of the environment which will often take around twelve months. When your school has only been guaranteed twelve months of life, you do not have that luxury. So I began the audit – looking at all those areas of strength that could be built on and mentally tagging all those areas for possible removal or serious modification and then making a start while my understanding was still developing and evolving.

THE STUDENT REPRESENTATIVE COUNCIL (SRC)

One area that really surprised me was the active, committed and talented young people who comprised the Student Representative

Council. Rather than a passive, obsequious group of title collectors, here was a group of articulate, well-organised go-getters, passionate about seeing their school survive and thrive. They could articulate exactly what was not working at 'Tempy', talked glowingly about the school's glory days when either they or their older siblings had enrolled and were quite demanding of me as to what I was going to do about restoring the school to this status. I loved this group and spent as much time with them as possible. They energised me and their naïve enthusiasm and optimism spurred me along. They would throw themselves into marketing discussions, advise about ways to improve the look of the school, address behavioural issues and turn up and contribute to the many working bees on the weekend.

EARLY STUDENT ACHIEVEMENTS

There are always some student achievements that stand out in your mind as a school leader and when you are trying to promote a school you search out, hang onto and sometimes 'embellish' these stories within your marketing.

We had a young lad, Andrea, who had a prodigious capacity for science, mathematics and spelling. In my first year he won a number of prestigious academic medals and I was so proud of him as I joined Andrea's family and my fellow Principals, many from the state's largest and most elite independent schools for the awards ceremony in the city. As we, a group of school leaders, watched our beloved and predominantly 'Aspie' kids, (Asperger's Syndrome, now Autism Spectrum Disorder) students walk awkwardly but excitedly across the stage, I could not have been happier. Both Andrea and his family became long-term supporters of TC. I loved the way our students applauded loudly and enthusiastically when Andrea's achievements were read out that day and at many subsequent assemblies over his time with us. Andrea's prodigious academic achievements, winning six medals in total, were instrumental in demonstrating to our TC community that students with strengths, passion and unusual talents could not only be nurtured and developed, but would be genuinely celebrated by our students and the broader community.

I was delighted to learn that Andrea has gone on to complete a Bachelor in Computer Studies with Honours and a Bachelor of Electrical Engineering with Honours from Latrobe University. Exceptional outcomes from an exceptional young man, who benefited from a unique educational experience.

Andrea with his swag of medals

Later that first year, Michael, a very capable engineering student, built his own incredibly impressive working model of a steam engine at home using his father's lathe. In a narrow academic sense, Michael was not exceptional but his out-of-school passion and talent, supported by his parents, was warmly embraced as valid as accomplishments achieved within the school. This validation and serious recognition of the amazing things students were undertaking outside school became an early hallmark of a TC education.

Michael and the Honourable Steve Herbert with his working model steam engine

CAMPS

Prior to the end of my first momentous term, I started to see Sally conducting camp meetings for next year. There were meetings to decide activities, meetings to discuss the menu, meetings to discuss sleeping arrangements, meetings to discuss the nightly entertainment, a meeting to bring in and check your equipment. Fancying myself as a bit of a camp efficiency expert, I asked Sally if it might not be possible to fulfill some of these functions at the same time.

'No,' she said, 'camp meetings build the excitement, sense of expectation and remind the students that might be thinking about leaving about all the fun they would miss out on. Besides that, we are showing that we are serious about student voice!' Then I understood, the anticipation of an event can be as enjoyable as the event itself. Good call, Sally.

COMMUNITY ENGAGEMENT

To engage our current parents, we ran a number of working bees per term, where we worked alongside parents, students, College Council members, staff and the family members of all of these groups, to rebuild the school and our sense of community. We painted, sewed costumes, cleaned, gardened, landscaped, moved furniture, built and repaired equipment. I still have many positive memories of these working bees. There were always lots of breaks to socialise and talk about the school and for me to share the plans of what we wanted to achieve by working together. The day would always finish with a sausage sizzle. They were not always cost effective in terms of physical output, but they were lots of fun. It was reassuring to know that there were others who were very keen to roll their sleeves up and get involved and who cared passionately about the success of the school.

Sally was the master of getting parents, grandparents, students and assorted others into the school to make costumes for our various plays and eisteddfods. I am not sure how Sally managed to run our small school almost single-handedly, while simultaneously running a sweat shop of volunteers whipping up bright costumes on sewing machines in the middle of the floor of the Resource Centre for many weeks in the lead-up to an event. (Think of a library, but louder and more interactive with far fewer books.)

THE SWIM SPORTS

I still have no idea why in Australian schools, in spite of the rhetoric about apparently needing to focus every minute on improving our allegedly declining literacy and numeracy results, that we privilege a whole day on swimming, athletics and half a day on cross country.

Swimming is done well by a few rare students and those who are actually squad swimmers are so much faster as to make the competition itself meaningless for victor or the vanquished. It also creates the potential for a totally inappropriate focus on body image to the degree that often only about 20% of students actually take part. These really do seem legacies of a wartime era of schooling of publicly testing the students' mettle, with little regard for their self-esteem.

What is our preoccupation with these events?

Instead of doing traditional House swimming, we took only those students who wanted to go to the Melbourne Sports and Aquatics Centre. We did specify that the minimum participation was a leisurely two-lap stroll around Albert Park Lake which was about 10km in total and was a great opportunity for staff to chat with students. Those who wanted to compete could have their times officially recorded for use in regional competitions, while the majority played games, and challenged their fear of heights on the diving boards and ten-metre diving tower. This became a regular feature of the school calendar that was looked forward to by the vast majority of students as an enjoyable and bonding experience and students chose to be involved to the degree that they wished.

Sometimes care = time

Never underestimate the power of relationship and personal connection. It is too easy to let these interactions slide, particularly when you as a leader are under time pressure. Consider carefully what your priorities are and consider privileging time spent with people and building deeper relationships ahead of having all your jobs done. Do you really want to be remembered as the leader who always kept their email inbox under control and who had great processes, or the person who always put people and relationships first?

While I know this principle, I have certainly not always practised this, but I also know that when I have not, it has been to the detriment of those around me. Awareness precedes change... be gentle with yourself.

INTERNATIONAL STUDENTS' PROGRAM

One of the more pleasant discoveries on my appointment was finding that we had an international students' program that was thriving. The three-person department of Angela, Margaret and Kim was a formidable team. Given that their fifty students at the start of my appointment represented around a fifth of the school population, the fees from which basically kept the school viable in those early years, this area warranted a lot of my attention. The international students contributed an enormous amount to the cultural capital of the school, and we were always very lucky to have students from around ten different nationalities, rather than being dominated by students from China as so many neighbouring schools were. Even our prospective Chinese parents sought us out, as a broader population ensured that their children would not fall into the habit of speaking primarily their own language and instead were more likely to mix with other students and gain a genuine international education.

I am courting the international market by being 'exceedingly cooperative' with the international students' centre within the department. They love my international students' coordinator who is a great operator, a real mum who deeply cares for but is quite strict with 'her' students. Our international numbers are holding at around 55 which is fantastic and in some ways is keeping the school afloat. We are contemplating a trip to China or Vietnam later in the year in order to keep these placements coming as they generally need two years' lead time. If our marks go down, which I don't believe they will (at least this year as we have a strong Y12) we could potentially lose this market.

Written during a SWOT analysis (Strengths, Weaknesses, Opportunities and Threats) prepared for College Council at the end of my first year.

Our International Program was an exemplar used by the Victorian Education Department and there were also huge potential benefits for local students from this program. Our classroom staff were adept at encouraging the local and international students to mix during class activities, but unfortunately few students crossed the cultural divide and became truly integrated into local life. In later years we were given permission to take on students from a younger age, twelve rather than the former age of sixteen, and this did have more promise as they had greater time to integrate without the pressure of senior studies and trying to integrate into existing social groupings.

Travelling overseas each year to 'market' TC to international students and their families in China and Japan was always a challenging but rewarding experience. While I had travelled as a tourist through many parts of Asia, this regular interaction certainly expanded my global perspective as an educator for which I am still grateful.

The schedules were inevitably gruelling, and trying to explain a student-empowered model to parents from predominantly authoritarian cultures was amusing. I am still not quite sure that my interpreters always accurately translated what I was saying, but rather told the parents what they wanted to hear. We did, however, continue to receive many referrals from previous students who had been students at TC. While I was not always confident of the academic standards of teaching in those early years, I was confident that the care this potentially vulnerable group of students would receive would be excellent.

A GREAT BUSINESS MANAGER IS A VITAL PIECE OF THE PUZZLE

As my undergraduate degree is in economics and accounting, I have a good understanding of financial management, but the Victorian Education Department has quite a bizarre accounting system that does not mirror any bookkeeping system that exists in industry. This can present quite a problem for ensuring high quality financial management in departmental schools as the wages are not really competitive to employ qualified accountants as business managers except in very large schools. Instead, schools often have to rely on people with limited training who have come up through the ranks within the system, often having started their career as the accounts payable clerk. While they usually do the technical aspects of their job quite well, having performed the role themselves at every level, their ability to advise a Principal on the running of a multi-million-dollar business is at best, limited. Given that Principals themselves often have scant financial knowledge, which is in itself problematic, it is not surprising that overall schools end up adopting very conservative mental models of finance, repeatedly doing what was done in previous years, or repeating how situations were handled in their previous schools. After all it worked safely then, so as long as we don't change things too much it should be safe for next year, too.

This conservative model locks all schools into patterns of 'rinse and repeat' or at best only looking at minor program tweaks, rather than proactively looking for financial opportunities, freeing up funds that could ultimately be used to benefit young people. This situation really does need to be sorted out and conventional accounting practices adopted in all department and systemic schooling systems to attract financial experts with fresh perspectives and new ideas to the education sector.

In Australia, this situation is not quite so dire in the independent system, which employs more conventional accounting practices and often has people with significant business experience on school boards, yet even there the salaries for business managers are often non-competitive with broader industry and prohibit people with true business flair from entering the sector.

Principals often lock the person with the title, Business Manager, into a mental role of 'keeper of the purse' and in many cases, the person who handles the 'scary financial stuff', which is often the principal's own weakness. In schools of the future, the finance manager handles these operational considerations, while the business manager works as a fully integrated member of the leadership group, continually rethinking and challenging how the school could adjust or reposition itself for more efficiency and better alignment with the strategic vision. The business manager should learn about learning, while exposing the leadership group to the opportunities producing demonstrated gains in the private sector. This will be quite a controversial point, as there is often a hard line taken that 'schools are not, and should not, be commercial businesses'. I agree that they should not be profit makers, but the sector could most certainly benefit from adopting many business practices, such as customer engagement, customer relationship management, and productivity, research and innovation and culture management with the 'profits' returned to benefit students rather than shareholders. Educational leaders do have to be careful to keep a check on this relationship, as commerce has a habit of consuming all before it, and can at times lead to ethically questionable outcomes, but nor should we lock ourselves off from talent, expertise and potential new ways of working simply because we are scared to even entertain possibilities. We need all the good ideas we can get to improve the lives of young people as rapidly as possible.

I was enormously fortunate to have Tony, a skilled Business Manager with significant public service experience. Together with the leadership team we were able to take calculated financial risks that other less experienced business managers might have been unwilling to take. When I was considering restructuring how classes and year levels were composed, he could quickly appreciate the financial and human relation implications as well as the learning impacts. Tony was also vital in keeping the 'bean-counters in town' satisfied that as a school we knew what we were doing and could succinctly convey that we had a financial path towards recovery.

The big things and the small things

Tony also took enormous pride in the school, oversaw facilities in those early years and had done a tremendous job keeping the school painted, clean and looking as presentable as possible, in spite of significant termite infestations, severe water leaks and aging infrastructure that was really in need of rebuilding. It was not unusual for Tony to come in on the weekends or very early in the morning after heavy rain, wearing his gumboots and mopping out water, to make sure that the school was safe and presentable for students. He would often comment laconically as he swished the mop down the hall after a rain event, 'You know, I used to manage ninety-eight staff and over a billion dollars in housing assets, don't you!' We were so fortunate to have Tony – he could do the high-order thinking, but did not see himself as too important to grab a mop when the situation demanded it.

There were several key personnel without any of which TC may not have survived – Tony was one of these and enabled me to concentrate on redeveloping the learning and operations. When you are trying to turn around a troubled school and money gets tight, painting and cosmetic maintenance are definitely NOT the things to cut back on. While there was much to do in terms of learning and behaviour, at least we had a clean, neat serviceable building.

Try to look prosperous, not in danger of closing

In those early days we had a significant number of excess teaching spaces. As a government school we were allocated cleaning and maintenance on a per student basis rather than on the physical area of the buildings. I received advice that we should close off certain wings of the school to reduce cleaning costs, but I felt that this was equivalent to admitting defeat. I would say to anyone that would listen – we will need all these spaces for the students we will have and we need these extra spaces so that students can personalise their learning. My advice to small schools with excess buildings is absorb the extra cleaning and maintenance costs and give students what they can't have in almost any other school – spaces to do stuff and spaces to claim and call their own.

'RED-LINE THE PAST'

One of the many things that would frustrate me in those early days was the staff's obsession with dredging up the past. 'We tried that once' was not a phrase I really appreciated, nor was the constant reference to the school by the students, staff and parents, some of whom were past students themselves, as 'Tempy' or 'Tempy Tech'. We had stopped being a tech school almost fifteen years earlier and the hangover from those days in contrast to the future-focused school we were trying to develop was unacceptable.

I said at an early staff meeting, in only a half-joking manner, 'Feel free to refer to the school as "Tempy"… on the last day you work here.' There was an awkward silence. I realised that I had made more of a point than I had intended to. I moved on with the meeting, but that was all it took to end that term among staff, unless they were playfully trying to bait me.

So important was it that staff let go of things that had or hadn't worked previously that I explained at a whole school assembly the accounting concept of 'red-lining the past'. In the days pre computers, an accountant might tally a long list of debits and credits and find the balance out by just a small margin. After checking for gross errors, they would rule a red line under the list and make a one-off adjustment to bring the totals into balance, because it was simply uneconomical to go through all the transactions to find the small transcription error of a few dollars. From this point the accounting process could move forward, acknowledging that there had been errors in the past but from now on things were in balance. While I explained that as a community, we all needed to 'red-line the past', the night before I had arranged for the maintenance person to paint a 40cm thick red line on the ground at the three gateways used by students, staff and the community. It was hard to miss and was a daily reminder that we were leaving the past behind at the gate and entering the grounds with a future-focused mindset.

Some staff, families and students understandably expressed that the red line representing a 'new school' was disrespectful to the many positive contributions and achievements of those who had gone before. Many staff had been there for more than ten, twenty, and in two cases more than forty years. Was this a rejection of them and their contribution? My counter claim was that if we didn't adopt this approach, we would *only* have historic memories and no viable future.

Having now spoken to many past students dating back almost to Templestowe's inception, the students' overall perceptions are strongly correlated to their specific years of attendance and the school's fortunes at that time. I developed a narrative – like any history, there have been good times and bad times, but if we want to have a chance at a future we need to move on and leave the past behind.

We placed the following extract on the school's website under the heading 'The TC story so far...'

> After individually interviewing all staff members, speaking to College Council, students, parents and members of the local community the first step was obvious. We as a community needed to "red line the past", and not look back. This is not to say that what had gone before was bad or wrong, indeed there have been many brilliant moments in TC's history, but trying to forever recapture the school's glory days was holding us back. That is why you will not currently find much of the school's previous history on this website. However, if you happen to be a past student, parent or staff member we still want to stay in contact and support you, so please get in touch.

We ended up hosting a number of open days, reunions and individual tours for past staff and students over the years and once the school was back on its feet and particularly after it began being featured for its innovation in state newspapers and on television, many past staff and parents expressed their delight at what their old school had become.

Is there something in your school's history holding it back?

Sometimes you do have to do something physical that symbolically severs the past from the future so people can move on.

It might be the result of community trauma or some particularly significant incident or event that is holding the school community in an old mindset. One school I worked with had been terribly impacted by bushfires, with many school families losing their homes and a number of parents and staff losing their lives in defence of their homes. Ten years had passed, yet the school culture was still being held in a traumatised state and was seemingly unable to move forward. A potential solution offered was to host a commemorative event to coincide with the impending ten-year anniversary of the fires, with the construction of a peace garden incorporating a walking bridge over a water feature, respectfully recognising a permanent connection with the past but a crossing over into a new state.

Is there something that you as a school community need to 'redline' and let go of?

Chapter Four

CREATIVE MARKETING STRATEGIES

EVERY DAY IS OPEN DAY

Having been appointed at the start of Term 4, I was told that the first thing we needed to focus on was preparing for Open Day like every other school in our area did, to try and attract students. There was a 'death story' circulating – last year the staff attending on the night significantly outnumbered the prospective parents. I did not feel that I personally could stomach such a demoralising situation and feared what a repeat of this experience would do to staff and community confidence which was in the very early stages of recovery. Once the message is out that a school is dying, it is hard to correct the perception. Instead, we decided that at TC 'Every day was Open Day'. If the public had a perception that the school environment was out of control, how would bringing them in after school hours – when only select students were there and only the best work was on display – alter that perception?

So instead, we offered tours directly with me, the Principal, whenever it suited parents. Enrolment interviews were so vital that no activity was more important than a parental meeting and we held them whenever it suited parents, whether that be at 7am or 8pm to accommodate parental working hours. We encouraged prospective families to ideally tour during the day when they could see the school in full swing. At that stage I could not guarantee what visitors might encounter so I would preface the tour with a comment such as 'This is a real school with real students. It is not like an open for inspection where you put away all your dirty washing in a cupboard. I cannot guarantee what you will see, but it will be "real" and we are all on a journey to become a great school.' My logic was that if we did 'burn' a family then at least we would spread the risk and burn them one at a time, whereas if we had a traditional Open Day and it did not go well, we may be irrevocably damaged.

As it turned out, parents were appreciative of the ninety minutes that I would spend with the family, first of all talking to the young person with their parents present for around thirty minutes about what their interests were, their hopes and dreams for their ideal education and what they hoped to do when they finished. This was then followed by a site tour, where I would give far greater emphasis on the aspects I felt would appeal to the young person. It is no use spending too long showing the sporty kid the music and art facilities, but instead talking about the lunchtime access to the weights gym and mentioning that we had students on a roster who would loan out sporting equipment at lunchtime. Likewise, for the art-orientated student, we would spend time sitting in the mezzanine level of the art room and explaining that without year levels they would not be held back by the students who really had no interest in art and instead could learn from working alongside older students. Because we had so much unused space, even younger students could have their own art studio cubical, 'just like at university', that they could leave set up with their work and continue working on it alongside fellow committed artists before, after school or whenever they had a free moment.

Make your first encounter with parents a personalised and positive one

It is always far easier to deal with a difficult situation involving a student, if the first time you have met their parents or guardians the atmosphere has been positive and relaxed. It is worth the time to get to know one another and if possible, to jot down some personal notes afterwards that you can brush up on before any subsequent meeting.

TEST OUT YOUR IDEAS WITH PROSPECTIVE FAMILIES

I also used these one-on-one family tours to test out ideas I was thinking about implementing, and experimented with the best language with which to sell. 'Would you mind if I ran an idea past you? I have been thinking about the possibility of students being allowed to pick their own learning mentor, rather than just being allocated to Mr X or Ms Y. Do you think that would make a positive difference to how you would feel about school?' This enabled me to both test how valuable parents and students found the idea, but also how to best communicate concepts that were just in the ideation phase. People liked to be taken into my confidence and they could see that we were on a clear growth and development trajectory. When we were on the tour, I was not selling what was already in place, but a vision of what we would become. Repeating this so often also helped to evolve and solidify my own vision for the school. In the end I could clearly see what we would one day become and my full-time job became a case of pointing out and correcting anything I saw or experienced that did not fit in with that vision. It was certainly not a static vision but one that adapted as I and the school community grew.

Often while conducting these interviews, I could sense the parents' excitement at the ideas I presented but there was a hesitancy of committing their child's longer term academic future to a school that could potentially close. To overcome this and reduce the magnitude of the decision they were making, I would explain that the concept of enrolling a student for six years was an old narrative and that we understood that it might be right for one or two years and that the student's needs might change. I would say, 'From our perspective, if 'Stacey' stays six months or six years, we will do our very best to support her for her time with us and she will always be regarded as a part of TC.'

Some parents felt that they thought TC might be right for one of their children but not another. I would say that schools used to operate on the assumption that 'if you get the first, you get the rest' and you will hold them for six years, deliberately emphasising the transactional, production-like model of traditional schooling, whereas the new model was to tailor each child's schooling to their particular needs. My response – 'In fact, it is sometimes better to have siblings in different schools so that they can develop their own personality independent of their brother or sister.' I would tend to emphasise this where I sensed a particularly dominant sibling and could see the relief wash over the face of the usually younger sibling, excited by the prospect of being able to forge their own identity and not be referred to as X's younger brother. In talking with students, many expressed that they really disliked when teachers made sibling references, often comparing them academically or even in terms of physical resemblance to other siblings. The same feedback came from students whose parents worked at the school. So strong and consistent was this reaction that we banned staff from referring to a sibling unless the student first initiated the discussion. At TC, each person had the right to be their own person, free from family baggage or preconception.

DOING TRADITIONAL SCHOOL, ONLY BETTER

Initially the focus of our advertising was around being another good conventional school, only smaller. We openly embraced our size and focused on the advantages of being small, finding several research papers that indicated that students in small schools often had a better experience particularly in terms of student involvement in co-curricular activities and feelings of connectedness compared to those students attending larger schools. We extensively quoted the metaanalysis of Kathleen Cotton's study 'School Size, School Climate, and Student Performance,' (*Close-Up* Number 20, 1996, Portland, Oregon) who reviewed 31 studies researching the relationship between small schools and academic achievement, where students in small schools performed equal to or better than their larger school counterparts. We would try to offer the best of being part of a small independent-style school, perhaps without the glamourous facilities, but at a bargain, government school price.

I was very uncomfortable with the idea that the new school should be focused on me. Sally, however, had other ideas! She said that having my face on the advertising was not about me but instead providing a reason for people to at least consider that things might be changing. She was quite right. So was born the cringeworthy tag line…

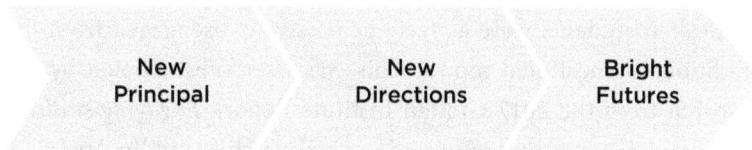

| New Principal | New Directions | Bright Futures |

Ten years in the leadership of top performing state and independent schools has taught me what parents want…. a disciplined learning environment where teachers know and care for each student and are willing to spend the time working with the family to maximise their potential and help them set and achieve their goals. I commit to offering long-term stability in leadership, creativity and passion in curriculum design and delivery.

I even started taking online lessons in Mandarin Chinese, so that I could say at least a few sentences of welcome to families from a Chinese background. The school had two separate Chinese language schools operating each weekend, and I was envious that they had far more students enrolled than we did. The lady who ran one of the Chinese schools was lovely and very influential within the large local Chinese community and was a great supporter of what we were trying to achieve. She even secured a radio interview and helped organise advertising on local Chinese radio. Eventually she admitted to me, 'The Chinese community is interested in what you are doing but they will only consider enrolling after the students' marks on external exams improve.' It was a classic Catch 22 – without the hard-working and academically oriented Chinese students we would not improve our results significantly within the time frame required for survival.

We needed a different strategy.

What about those students who for whatever reason did not 'fit' elsewhere? My experience at the time told me that at least a third of Australian students were actively or passively disengaged from the traditional educational model. This was later substantiated by the research from the 2017 Grattan Institute Report *'Engaging students creating classrooms that improve learning'* which found 'In Australia, many students are consistently disengaged in class and approximately 40% are unproductive in a given year.'

We had started to attract a few students who fitted this description and they seemed to have re-engaged and to be doing okay. Their parents also seemed to be far more willing to try something new, given the old system had already failed them. So, the reality is that the new TC journey did not start with saving lost educational souls as its foundational purpose, but rather so that the school could survive. This is nowhere near as romantic, and may even be disillusioning to some, but it is honest. Over time, however, I grew to see the enormous value of providing a high-quality educational alternative for young people whose needs were not being met by the existing school system, and it has become my passion as well as my life's work.

NICK THE COFFEE MAN – A UNIQUE MARKETING INITIATIVE!

We knew that we needed to start changing our reputation and do so quickly. I approached a mobile barista called Nick the Coffee Man and with the local school leaders' permission, we visited our five main feeder primary schools during school drop-off times offering free coffee to parents and staff if they would just take a school brochure. It was a little out there, but I had done a cold calling job when I was a university student, and felt that if nothing else, prospective parents and the primary staff whose opinion often impacted significantly on the choices of a secondary school could see my smiling face and see that I was keen. I was also pretty sure that doing something a little out there might get some positive word of mouth flowing.

PROSPECTING FOR PRECIOUS GEMS

For a brief period before starting my teaching qualification I was recruited by a family member into selling insurance and other financial products for one of Australia's largest life insurance companies. This was a particularly challenging role for me. Initially I tried selling to the 'mums and dads' market where most people selling insurance start out. Unfortunately, as I was under twenty-five, driving a sports car and was still wearing the expensive suits purchased during my brief stint as an accountant in Melbourne, I did not have the relatability and reliability-vibe of my generally portly and jolly 'family-man' colleagues. What I did have, though, was an accounting degree which at that time was very rare in the financial services industry. I switched from selling to the 'mums and dads' to professionals and small business owners, who appeared to like the more showy, quick-talking and qualified me. I undertook the sales training which was quite theoretical and evidence based. They explained ratio analysis and process of turning leads into qualified leads into meetings into sales. They taught about the psychology of both the buyer and seller and how to overcome buyer resistance with various sales tactics.

My career as an insurance salesman was limited and while quite lucrative financially, I developed significant 'phone resistance', a phenomenon experienced by many telemarketers that can build up after facing too many rejections. For several years after this time I had difficulty talking comfortably on the phone much less making any kind of unsolicited call. I also had an ethical dilemma in that I could only sell products that I knew from my financial background to be high-quality products and were genuinely in the clients' best interests and at the time these were quite limited. When I discovered that I could hear the word 'redundancy' across a crowded room at a party and that person immediately became a prospect, I knew it was time to get out. While my sales career was short-lived, the training was amongst the most valuable formal education I have ever received. One comment that friends and foe alike would often level at me, generally in jest, was that I could sell anything to anyone. It is a claim that still challenges me to a degree. Provided one has a good product, is the ability to help people commit to something that will benefit them such a bad thing?

I explained to the office staff just how important their role was in terms of first impressions. We adjusted some administrative staff roles to ensure prospective families as well as the existing community were met with a smiling and happy face each day. The office staff were trained to always obtain contact information from prospective parents as a top priority. Once I had contact information the data was entered on a prospect sheet and the hunt began. There were only three ways of getting off the prospect list – either enrol, my decision to drop the enrolment after meeting the family or when the parent told me to please, never call again. Even in the latter case, even once the student had commenced attending another school, the parents would be scheduled for a follow-up call in six months to check in and see how the new school was working out. On a few occasions the parent admitted that the new school was not what they thought it would be and they would then come for a second tour of TC. At worst, they would say, 'Boy, you are persistent,' which still felt slightly positive.

A friendly face makes all the difference

In my current role I visit a lot of schools and I am often amazed at how many of the frontline staff appear jaded, overworked, unfriendly or plain unhelpful. Such frontline behaviour would never be tolerated in any commercial business or at least one which hoped to grow. I have spoken to a number of teachers, even principals, who have admitted that they too are afraid of their own office staff. Reception and registrar are two vital roles where a school that hopes to grow cannot tolerate people who do not possess excellent, warm customer service skills. If you find your school in this situation and you can possibly stretch the finances, redeploy them immediately to a role that does not have outward public contact while you then manage the fall-out and work out what to do with them next. Often these staff can still be quite connected to the community, trading in gossip, and need to be given clear directives not to communicate in such a way as to compromise the school's reputation or else face formal disciplinary action. Every negative interaction could be the cost of an enrolment that over a potential thirteen years of schooling could be worth anything from $130K to well over half a million dollars if that empty place is never filled. And frontline people can have more than a hundred interactions per day! When you think about the role in those terms, it becomes logical to spend money on training in quality frontline service. In those early days I did go so far as to have a few friends, both educators and non-educators, come through as 'mystery shoppers', then report back on what their prospective enrolment experience was like.

Prospective students were grouped into hot, warm, cool and 'No Go' folders. After teachers had left for the day, I would settle in with my prospect lists and start the calls. Each contact with a family elicited more information which was then added to the file. This was a very draining process, and some nights I could not face the task. At other times I would quite seriously have to jump up and down, slap myself in the face a few times and psych myself up for the task ahead. My time in sales had taught me that this process was not about feelings, my impressions of who would sign on and who wouldn't, but about playing the numbers. The more calls I made, the more enrolments we got – it was as simple as that.

Marketing for enrolments is a numbers game

If you are a school seriously in need of enrolments, you need to play the numbers and try to keep your own personal feelings of dread at making prospecting calls in check. This concept can seem repellent to educators as we live so much of our lives in the relational space, but the reality is that companies have built fortunes on this sales methodology. You can spend ages with a prospective family only to be disappointed at the last moment and find later that they really liked you as a person and as such did not want to give an outright 'no' and disappoint you. Likewise, some parents may initially seem quite guarded, even dismissive and yet go on to become highly involved and supportive members of the community. Make your targets for the number of prospective family calls you will make each week, which is one of the few aspects of the enrolment process that you can control and stick to it.

In those early days, when the school was not yet what any of us would want it to be, we would occasionally have parents walk in the front door to enrol simply because we were their local school. Sometimes they were newly arrived migrant families and it would quickly become apparent that their child was quite academic and that the family had high aspirations. I would be twinged with guilt enrolling their child, as I felt their child was almost 'too good for the school'. I knew that what the parents really wanted was a more traditional school with like-minded academically focused peers, teachers focused on maximising scores and that our culture was not that. What to do? We were desperate for the enrolments and so in the end I would take the enrolment but then endeavour to put in a range of personal supports with staff to give the student specialised atten- tion. Many of these students ended up doing amazingly well. I put some of their disproportionate success down to a significant boost in learning confidence when capable students develop a self-perception of being relatively 'exceptional', whereas had they attended a higher performing school they may well have ended up feeling rather 'average'. Over time as the learning culture of the school improved, this became less of an issue, but we would often have to clarify for walk-in-families that we were not the average school and that they should look around and ensure we were the type of school that they wanted for their young person.

A SCHOOL FOR THE QUIRKY

We started looking at which primary feeder schools saw the world a little differently and wondered if we could form a relationship that would see their students and parents referred to us. We found the Hurstbridge Learning Co-op, The Village School and the local Montessori school. I contacted the principals and asked if I could visit. I subsequently attended school plays and sports days to hand out ribbons and conducted talks for the staff about where our new style of schooling was headed. All principals were highly supportive of what we were trying to achieve and explained that it would also benefit them if they were able to demonstrate to their existing and potential parents that there was a secondary school option sympathetic and aligned to the general ideals of these alternative primary schools. The fact that we were also a government school and hence at a far lower cost made the offer even more appealing.

We also reached out to representatives from the home-schooling movement. For many years I had admired what home-schooled students and their parents had been able to achieve and felt that if we worked together, we could get the best of both worlds. To prospective home-schooled parents I made the offer – let's look at dual enrolment and if your young person gets something from the experience including access to specialist facilities as well as making a few friends, then that's a bonus. I coined the phrase that TC was like 'a supported form of home-schooling'. I had one parent enrol saying that it might be for six days or six months, depending on how it worked. I am pleased to say that young Harry was still at TC six years later and grew into one of the most delightful students I ever worked with.

A fellow principal passed along a rumour that a group of parents from the Montessori community were looking to start their own Montessori secondary school. I met two members of the steering committee, Victoria and Alina, and asked why would you want to start a school and have to charge parents fees when you could run a Montessori school within our school, financed by the government? They jumped at the opportunity for further discussion. At the time the Department of Education was feeling bruised by an alternative school whose community had gone a little rogue, so they had placed an embargo on considering any new proposals for Montessori, Steiner and Sophia Mundi integrated schools. This was a problem, that on reflection, could be overcome by calling the new Montessori school an Erdkinder stream. Erdkinder means 'children of the land' and was familiar enough code for Montessori parents to know what it was but to be outside the wording of the embargo. We went ahead and started what to the best of our knowledge was the world's first and only Erdkinder Stream. I pulled my head down and waited for the metaphorical slap to the back of the head to come from the region or central office for my transgressions. This was an almost innate response cultivated from my schooling days whenever I did anything wrong... but nothing came. I became emboldened. Just how much *could* we get away with?

ADVERTISING

During my time at TC, the local paper was still widely read and so we spent a considerable amount on print advertising. This was far more than most schools would normally spend – around $40K per year in the first few years. My theory was that if we were going to die, it would not be because people did not know who we were and what we were about. One of my more audacious schemes was to get an elephant on site at the school. It would be done under the guise of the Working with Animals program, but really it was to be a marketing stunt. The tag line for the eventual news article was going to be 'We think BIG at Templestowe College'. I reached out to a circus which had the last working elephant in Australia by the name of Saigon. We agreed to pay them $10K for the day and set a date. Unfortunately, they checked their insurance and said that it was outside their Occupational Health and Safety cover. The kids were disappointed, I was gutted.

Saigon, Australia's last circus elephant, on the day of her retirement.
Can't you imagine a big Red TC on that belly?

As the school property was landlocked with the entrance located at the end of a court and no road frontage, even letting the community know that we existed was a challenge. I genuinely felt that we had quickly developed some pockets of greatness, but how could we get this message out there? I had visions of me head-locking local students on their way past our front door heading to neighbouring schools and dragging them into the school for a look. I felt that if they saw what was happening, we might have a chance of winning them over. I resisted the urge.

It was about this time that an advertising company approached schools and was offering them advertising space on the side panels of bus stop shelters. Whether deliberate or not, a neighbouring state school principal of a large and thriving school authorised advertising at every bus stop along the main route leading to our school. Pressure can breed paranoia, but our students, staff and parent community were incensed, and felt it was a hostile act. In a strange way this event galvanised the community and it was reassuring to see some passionate support for what we were building being voiced by the school. I suggested to a group of middle-school boys that I would first try the diplomatic approach of calling the principal, rather than taking up their well-meaning offer to deface the posters with their permanent markers. The call to the offending principal was pleasant enough, and they agreed to have the signage removed. It did, however, remind me that while there is collegiality and supposed cooperation between government school principals, no one likes a change in status. We had moved relatively quickly from being the no-threat, basket-case school to an emerging player in the local area.

While the Department would like to consider that schools operate in collegial networks there is most certainly competition not only for students, but for the *highest performing* students. Once relativities are established there can be collaboration, but as soon as one school seeks to innovate in a significant way the defensive and reactive walls go up quite quickly. Only fixed school boundaries where the best school is your local school as occurs in Finland can stop this phenomenon and support genuine professional collaboration, but removing 'parental choice' in Australia would be very difficult from a political perspective. In spite of being the richest country in the world as measured by median wealth[*], the rise of low fee independent schools has been a significant factor in Australia becoming the third-worst country of the thirty-three OECD nations for educational equity.

---

[*] https://ceoworld.biz/2021/07/25/which-countries-are-the-richest-based-on-median-wealth-per-adult/

As well as trying to attract student enrolments at Year 7, it was important to simultaneously try to grow the school at all year levels otherwise we would become a very small school indeed as our shrinking cohorts flowed through the next six years. This meant trying to draw in students who were either already in schools or were home-schooled. My observation is that even when a student has struggled with a conventional school program in primary school, parents hold out hope that their journey through a traditional secondary school program will in some ways be different. The reality is that such difficulties of a poor fit are usually magnified without the single teacher contact and care point of the primary setting. This meant that there were many students in the early secondary years of our traditional neighbouring schools that could potentially be drawn to the far more flexible and student-centred TC program.

Rather than pitching to 'average students' who were unlikely to be drawn from an environment that was working moderately well for them, I felt that we were more likely to get interest from those who were disengaged or whose needs were currently not being well met. Thus we led with advertising campaigns like:

Be a name, not a number!

Each student comes to school with their own story!

At Templestowe we appreciate that all students have different needs, skills, talents and aspirations. Everyone comes to school with their own story, yet in most schools this personal element goes largely ignored. At Templestowe College we believe that the future of education will see schools move from a one-size fits all curriculum to an 'a la carte' educational experience, where the student and their family tailor the educational program to THEIR particular needs. How can

Templestowe manage to deliver this when other schools struggle to do so? Our smaller size enables us to be flexible and adaptable. We are not driven rigidly by the timetable, all staff are committed to implementing our vision, and this philosophy is driven by our Leadership Team.

– Peter Hutton, Principal

22,000 Reasons to consider Templestowe College

(This was a challenge to the 60% of our local parents who were sending their children to private schools, many of whom would be far more suited to a flexible learning environment.)

What else could you do for your son or daughter and their broader education with the $22,000 many parents are outlaying EACH YEAR for private school fees?

- Regular overseas travel showing them the real world?
- Pay their Uni fees instead and not leave them holding a massive student debt?
- Buy them a new car with all the latest safety features?
- Put the more than $130,000 into a significant down payment on their first home.

Are you really getting value for money? Check out a very REAL alternative.

- Laptop program at Years 7-12
- Student selected Learning Mentor
- Personalised curriculum at Years 7-12
- A small caring environment
- Three-year VCE & VCAL program
- Where learning can be fun.

@ Templestowe College Students Drive their own Learning

It seems today that society tries to label us, tell us how we should act, what we should think and generally try to make us into something we are not.
At TC, students have the opportunity to be themselves, explore their interests and passions, express their opinions and contribute directly to how the school runs. If you are looking for a school where you can be yourself, have great relationships with staff and learn alongside others who have a plan for where they are going, then TC might be just what you are looking for.

Peter Hutton, Principal

7 Cypress Avenue, Lower Templestowe 3107
Tel. 9850 6333 Fax. 9852 0728
templestowe.co@edumail.vic.gov.au

Not happy at School? Life is too Short!

Adolescence is too short to be stuck in a school that does not recognise you for who you are, your unique talents, your quirky personality or even know your name. At Templestowe College we accept that students are individuals and want different things from their education. We actively encourage students to drive their own learning and offer them genuine choices to personalise their learning. We have helped students who are inventors and scientists find a place where their talents are appreciated. We have helped artists, dancers and musicians to thrive. We have helped those who have felt anxious, isolated or bullied in their previous school to find peace and establish new friendships. We have a program that allows academically talented kids to race ahead rather than have their enthusiasm crushed. If this sounds like an environment that would benefit you then contact our Principal, Peter Hutton for a confidential discussion or personalised tour.

Templestowe College
Cypress Avenue, Lower Templestowe
Tel.: 9850 6333 Fax: 9852 0728

templestowe.co@edumail.vic.gov.au

7 Cypress Avenue, Lower Templestowe 3107
Tel. 9850 6333 Fax. 9852 0728
templestowe.co@edumail.vic.gov.au

Find your smile @ Templestowe College

Adolescence is too short to be stuck in a school that does not recognise you for who you are, your unique talents, your quirky personality or even know your name. At Templestowe College we accept that students are individuals and want different things from their education. We actively encourage students to drive their own learning and offer them genuine choices to personalise their learning. We have helped students who are inventors and scientists find a place where their talents are appreciated. We have helped artists, dancers and musicians to thrive. We have helped those who have felt anxious, isolated or bullied in their previous school to find peace and establish new friendships. We have a program that allows academically talented kids to race ahead rather than have their enthusiasm crushed. If this sounds like an environment that would benefit you then contact our Principal, Peter Hutton for a confidential discussion or personalised tour.

Templestowe College
Cypress Avenue, Lower Templestowe
Tel.: 9850 6333 Fax: 9852 0728

templestowe.co@edumail.vic.gov.au

7 Cypress Avenue, Lower Templestowe 3107
Tel. 9850 6333 Fax. 9852 0728
templestowe.co@edumail.vic.gov.au

REACH OUT TO VISITORS AND VIPS

Nick Kotsiras was our local Member of Parliament. He approached me early on and arranged to visit the school. He explained that TC was the only government secondary school in his electorate and that he was very keen not to see it close. I almost fell off my chair. The first person outside the school who also had a vested interest and wanted to see the school succeed. Even though Nick was from the Liberal Party which was in opposition, he said that he would introduce us to a friend, Steve Herbert, who was the Labor Parliamentary Secretary for Education and invite him to also visit. Nick was annoyed that our neighbouring schools had each received significant rebuilding grants a few years earlier while due to our uncertain future, TC had received no money. The stark comparison between TC's forty-year-old buildings and the two state-of-the-art larger colleges less than four kilometres from us was also making student recruitment difficult. We were given support in preparing a grant submission which ultimately saw us receive a $3.5 million partial upgrade a few years later.

Extract from College Council Minutes

On Wednesday 2nd December, Templestowe College was delighted to host a visit from the Honourable Steve Herbert, State Member for Eltham and Parliamentary Secretary for Education. Steve was visiting at the invitation of our own Local Member of Parliament for Bulleen, the Honourable Nick Kotsiras, to hear about the many positive changes happening at the College, and spent almost two hours visiting classrooms, talking to students and discussing the future directions of education. At the conclusion of what was a challenging and forthright discussion with the former teacher, who now visits around twenty-five different schools per month, Steve made the comment that, "This school is on the cutting edge of education. I am very impressed with the College's innovative subjects and programs. Templestowe College certainly has a very positive feel about it."

This early interaction did teach me the value of bringing important visitors on site. I thought if I could extract an endorsement from them attesting to what we were trying to achieve, we might just get a few more enquiries and if the support was strong enough from people of influence, it could result in perhaps another year's reprieve from our impending execution. From that time on I made a habit of reaching out to at least six notable educators, politicians or influential people each term. Some took several attempts to snare, but persistence paid off. By the end of eight years, our list of visitors and VIPs to TC was a who's who of Australian and international educators. This proved not only to provide a sound base to our marketing but was also powerful in defending us from unwanted attention from the Department. When one of my Senior Education Improvement Leaders once told me he wasn't really sure about the benefits of individualised learning, I offered to connect him with Professor Yong Zhao from Kansas University 'because he seems to think the idea is pretty good and I am sure he would be interested to hear your concerns...'

BEING SEEN

Advertising can only go so far. 'Copy' is often written by marketers and I've discovered that people want to know if YOU as the leader of the school will back up your claims. This is where public relations comes in, being out there meeting with people face to face, one on one and in small groups. I think sometimes new principals think that they only need to be seen at the big gatherings, such as assemblies and key school events. If that is the case, why do we see presidents and prime ministers the world over pressing the flesh? No, we don't have camera crews and media entourages accompanying our every move, but people do talk and if for a moment you think you are beyond having a one-on-one discussion with a parent or taking individual interest in a student matter, then you are in for a Parent & Friend (rather ironically named) bashing. Regardless of the size of the school or fees paid, if you think you are 'too good' to get involved when required at the grassroots level you will be in for a world of hurt in the court of public opinion. I do appreciate that this is a very Australian phenomenon and will certainly not be true of all cultures.

For those first few years, I tried to be everywhere to increase the school's profile and create interest that might lead to an enquiry. Many of these tactics are not new, but it is important for the reader to know that we tried conventional strategies as well. I visited primary schools and met the principals, I attended the primary school plays, concerts and art exhibitions and asked if my presence could be mentioned. I did presentations for the School Councils on the future of education. We negotiated with the RSL to have our students read the ode at Anzac Day and Remembrance Day. I handed out medals at primary school sports days and had our student leaders run leadership sessions for primary school student leaders and gave talks to parent groups and Year 6 classes on getting over their fears of coming to secondary school. I tried where possible to see our own students off at the end of each day and welcome them by name each morning.

SOMETIMES IT'S THE SMALL WINS THAT GET YOU THROUGH

As a way to promote the school, one of the staff invited Michele Timms, Australian basketball legend, and several members of the Bulleen Boomers to visit Templestowe College to run a clinic with our senior girls and boys' basketball teams and also to run games and activities with the school at lunchtime.

In front of the school, Michele challenged me to a three-point shoot out competition with Australian basketball star Liz Cambage, who towered over me at 2.03m tall. I was extremely nervous and to be honest, did not want to embarrass myself too much in front of the school. Having spoken at assemblies about appropriate risk-taking and seizing opportunities, I could hardly say no. I was first up and all I kept repeating to myself was, 'Just hit the backboard. Just hit the backboard.'

Amazingly, I shot the first three-pointer and the kids went wild. Liz was impressed and went to the line, easily sinking her three-pointer. My turn again… 'Just hit the backboard…' and bam! Amazingly, TWO three-point shots in a row. The kids were shocked, but not half as much as I was. I started to hear staff and students who did not really know me say, 'Oh, I didn't know he was a basketballer.' I'm not!

Liz stepped up to the line and effortlessly sank her second shot. I stepped up to the line, I had nothing to lose already having acquitted myself beyond my wildest dreams, not having ever sunk two three-point shots in succession before.

Bam! THREE three-point shots in a row! Kids were screaming, I was in a state of shock. Divine intervention perhaps? Liz stepped somewhat hesitantly to the line, perhaps thinking this was a set-up or TV video prank, hit the rim and the ball bounced away…

Principal Peter Hutton had defeated Liz Cambage, current holder of the WNBA single-game scoring record with her fifty-three-point performance against New York Liberty on 17 July 2018, in a three-point shoot out competition!

I had the following photo blown up and put in the foyer, and if I was in a playful mood I would explain the story when giving school tours and say that I was waiting for my call-up to the WNBA.

Tongue in cheek, whenever there was a fire drill and students were told to leave their possessions in the classroom, I would calmly walk to the foyer, remove the picture and take it onto the oval. The kids would laugh and I would say, 'Not even a fire is going to take away this moment from me!'

My successful three-point shoot out competition against Liz Cambage

Chapter Five

'WHOSE EDUCATION IS THIS?'

THE 'BLAH' CURRICULUM

I despise curriculum, well most of it, anyway. It seems abhorrent to me that one human, faculty, State or National Education Department can prescribe what another human being will learn for 13,000 hours over thirteen years, when none of them knows what skills and knowledge the future will call for. We decided early on that we as staff would provide advice and guidance, but students would be given control over what they learnt. In reality, students have this choice anyway and frequently exercise that right by only engaging with the material and tasks presented to them in the most simplistic and superficial ways. There are some things that it is best to know and some skills such as reading, writing and basic numeracy that are of significant benefit, but really the list of mandatory things to be learnt should actually be quite small and most of that covered in the first half of primary school. Our aim was that the prescribed Victorian curriculum would be the fallback, the default, rather than the focus, and would only be pursued when students were not pursuing more interesting activities.

'IF YOU COULD LEARN ANYTHING IN THE WORLD, WHAT WOULD IT BE?'

We started with a simple question put to students, 'If you could study anything… in the world… what would it be?' After a little thought, the answer came back – art, dance, drama, textiles. Clearly the students had missed the point. I said, 'No, they are subjects. That's what you *think* you might be able to learn about in a school. Set your mind free – what would YOU really like to learn?'

Now this was potentially a dangerous question. The school was still shrinking with large cohorts of over 150 students graduating each year and incoming enrolments of less than fifty. Was this really the time to be expansionist? Should we be raising expectations of offering even greater subject choice that realistically given the current school structure could never be met?

When I looked at students who had the broadest range of learning opportunities, I saw two groups – those students in large schools with a secondary enrolment of 1500+ and home schoolers. In reality, those kids whose parents had for whatever reason decided or agreed to home school their child, had the greatest freedom – markets of one! TC at that time had junior cohorts so small (twenty-eight in the first year, forty-five in the second and seventy-five in the third) so that perhaps home schooling was a better mental framework on which to design and build our new school.

After pushing a little harder about what students REALLY wanted to learn, we got answers like computer gaming design, working with animals and building stuff. In reality the range of options suggested by students was unfortunately not all that broad. The system, and in particular, the media's portrayal through movies and sit-coms has only helped to reinforce the existing school paradigm from an early age. Perhaps influenced by two teacher-parents, our own daughters were playing schools from around three years of age, and quite a draconian form of education it was too!

Don't expect young people to have the answers to a new model of schooling

Sadly, don't have high expectations for unearthing creative new ideas when you ask young people how school should change. They inevitably don't know. It is their first time through the process. Motivated innovative educators who ask this question in more traditional school settings are inevitably disappointed. A student's view of school is limited to examples they have seen and their world view is one of having education done to them. The idea that any other way could exist is just too much of a stretch without support.

One method that we have found works is to ask students to write down their ideas on how school could be different and then explain that their contributions will be amalgamated with those of students and educators at other innovative schools and the collective genius of the crowd presented back to the whole group for discussion. This way you are able to seed the ground with loads of exciting ideas that can overcome students' stilted vision of schooling and trigger students' imaginations. Once students see what is possible, they are far better able to talk and expand on ideas that trigger their interest.

We collated the student requests and so were born our first non-traditional electives, Computer Gaming Design and Working with Animals. We added these to some already strong electives such as Art, Hospitality, Sport and a quick flip of Music from classical to a contemporary rock bands program and we were ready to go. We now had some significant student interest, but who was going to teach these newly devised electives? We already had an excess of staff due to our shrinking numbers and to be frank, those staff with the 'get up and go' had largely 'got up and gone', other than a handful of dedicated and unrealistically optimistic staff.

The inevitable effects of a shrinking pond

When a troubled school is contracting from over 1000 to 400 over a short timeframe, staff can see the writing on the wall. Those that can get out often do. This is particularly true for high-quality staff at lower ends of the salary bands which can result in an already cash-strapped school having a greater percentage of expert teachers which is VERY expensive while also reducing the number of excited, passionate and committed staff new to teaching to run activities at lunchtimes and after school. More experienced staff can potentially add great value in terms of subject expertise, pedagogical knowledge and wisdom, yet proportionally they tend to offer less by way of co-curricular activities which shrinking schools so desperately need.

Computer Gaming

I reached out to LaTrobe University and met a wonderful lecturer in Computer Gaming Design called Paul Taylor. We chatted on the phone for over an hour and I explained about TC and what we were trying to achieve in terms of supporting students to follow their passions. He very kindly offered to drop in once per week on his way home and teach our students and their quite nervous teacher. I will never forget the first day Paul turned up, torn-off shorts and old t-shirt and to me, he looked like he was about eighteen. Of course, he was the Computer Gaming Design Head of Faculty... how cool!

It was not always easy, particularly as students imagined the process of designing computer games to be far easier and quicker than what happens in reality. Many times I walked past the classroom and could see some students playing computer games in this class rather than building them. I consoled myself with the fact that at least they had the opportunity to learn what they wanted and were at least happy to be at school, many of them for the first time.

Working with Animals

In the Working with Animals program, Athena the Biology teacher was keen to do what she could to help the school survive – she also had great relationships with the students. She drove to the pet store and bought various rats, mice, guinea pigs, rabbits, interesting insects of various kinds and a snake! The laboratory in which the Working with Animals program was housed looked like it was falling down and had plaster missing from some of the roof. It stank incredibly and had poor ventilation… the kids loved it! It was their area and they were keen to show prospective students and their parents through the space. Few parents and prospective students escaped without a commemorative photo of a snake draped over their shoulders that we would email to them with a follow-up to their visit. From a marketing perspective, the Animals program was pure gold!

In terms of student academic outcomes, I did worry about what the students were really learning in our Working with Animals program and was tinged with guilt. Few had the academic capacity to go on and achieve the extremely high marks required to study veterinary science, although one of those early students certainly did end up becoming a veterinarian via a science pathway. What were students getting out of this program other than fun? Over time and with the benefit of hindsight those early students most certainly developed significant soft skills as well as significant organisational and leadership skills as they took on the total operation of the program. Most of the students in those early days were young. Many had come from their primary schools having been leaders and had already exercised significant levels of responsibility looking after other younger students. For our TC students, looking after animals fulfilled what

appeared like an innate need to care for something beyond themselves. Over time I saw that many students who were heavily involved
in the Working with Animals program went on to study and pursue
pathways in the caring, teaching and health care professions. At the
time I would say, 'Give a kid a rabbit to pat, and you have an enrolment.' And at that time, enrolments were exactly what was needed
for the school to survive.

A young Anna, who after her TC journey is now training as a paramedic

The common Year 7 satisfaction slide

It is well known that Year 7 student satisfaction takes a significant
dive after semester one of their move to secondary school. Students
are initially excited about coming to high school and being free of
the close supervision of predominantly the one classroom teacher.
Over time they find that, in fact, no adult looks after them, knows
or cares about them anywhere near as well as primary school. As the
smallest beings in the larger environment, their previous leadership

skills are generally not valued or recognised. Is it any wonder that confidence, happiness and engagement begin to slide?

Secondary schools need to find some way to harness and build upon the leadership that many young people in Year 7 displayed as leaders within their primary schools, rather than treating them as helpless beings. An animals program ensures that they are never the smallest creature in the school and provides them with an obvious way to show maturity and to care for something beyond themselves.

CATERING FOR THE HIGHLY ACADEMIC STUDENTS

To accommodate those few highly academically able students who were still at TC, we purchased a school subscription to a service called Your Tutor where the students could get one-on-one tutoring from a live Australian tutor from 3pm to 10.30pm every school night. While this represented a significant additional expense, neither Sally nor I wanted the school to be the barrier in the way of a student achieving their academic dreams. We could track the number of students utilising this service and while it wasn't high and possibly did not justify the cost, it did place the responsibility back on the students and gave an additional source of instruction and support besides their classroom teacher, who in some cases, was the only adult with this subject knowledge in the small school.

Many of our teachers voluntarily took a keen interest in helping our relatively few highly academic students, often providing one-on-one additional tutoring. Many of these students went on to achieve quite pleasing results in their senior studies, but then really excelled once they reached university. I attribute this success in a tertiary setting to the level of academic independence the students developed at TC and for their high level of learning confidence gained over six years that 'they were the brightest of the bunch'. This is often referred to as the Big-Fish-Little-Pond effect (BFLP) and has a strong evidence base.

CHOICE FROM YEAR 7

When trying to establish points of difference between TC and our neighbouring schools, I felt that students having some elective choice right from the time they started school in Year 7 would be attractive to prospective students and their families. As an arbitrary starting point, we felt it would be ideal if students controlled one third of their time at school (two electives of 3 × 75 minutes), while the remainder of the time was filled with the conventional curriculum. However in that first year with only two small Year 7 classes of fourteen, the number of options that students could have would be extremely limited. Students could effectively only have four choices. Having previously been Principal of a small independent school, I was aware of the benefits of putting the electives of a number of year groups in the same timetabling lines. So we looked at blocking the two Year 7 classes at the same times as the two Year 8 classes, which gave the students a potential eight electives. We then thought, why not combine with the three Year 9 elective classes as well, meaning we could offer fourteen potentially different electives at an economical price. We were then able to bring this number of elective classes down even further by increasing elective class sizes up to around twenty-four and put the money saved into buying significantly better equipment and resources for these electives. TC was one of few schools where class sizes in electives was larger than those of core classes. The reality was that student choice at TC started as much due to marketing, logistic and financial reasons as pedagogical ones.

These new electives raised the issue of increasing costs when the budget was already well into the red. In the Victorian State education system, schools are permitted to pass on the cost of materials or external service providers to parents. Commonly these fees are around forty to sixty dollars per subject, but there are no official limits placed on these costs. Our thinking was – what if we quadrupled this cost, what could that make possible? While there were questions raised by staff about a state school charging subject fees considerably more than those of our neighbouring government high schools, my comment was that 'people are not leaving because we are charging too much'. Indeed, we were only fifteen minutes from Kew, the suburb with the highest concentration of high-fee private schools in the southern hemisphere. A high price point was not our problem. What these higher subject fees did was to enable students to think of large and impressive projects. Rather than students building design and tech projects like a pencil case out of pine, our students used teak, merbau and jarrah to construct furniture. Rather than a small electronics kit, one of our students built a 1.8 metre Tesla coil that could throw a 10,000 volt spark 15 centimetres. Price was of little barrier and if needed, the school would foot the bill if the project was particularly impressive and we could keep it on display for some time. These projects were great showcases for what unique projects were possible for students to develop at TC.

Xavier Roberts and his 10,000 volt Tesla coil

ABOLISH YEAR 10

As we looked at how we were going to financially survive that first year, we accepted that we would be operating well into the red, but we needed to look at ways of cost saving. I started to consider what it meant to be a Year 10 student in the Australian education system. Across all schools, these students have some of the lowest satisfaction data of any year level and was a major exit point for TC students transferring to other schools. A theory I had is that when staff are allocated, we often allocate the 'best' teachers to Year 12, the next best, particularly the most engaging, to Year 7, then to Year 11 and the most robust, interpersonally able staff to cope with what many regard as the difficult Year 9 level. Where does that leave Year 8 and 10 students? While many teachers will teach Year 8 and 10 classes as part of their teaching load, in my opinion they often become the teachers' 'filler' classes. In Australia, Year 10 is that sad wasted year after the special Year 9 program designed to engage the disengaged and yet does not quite have the importance of the two-year senior certificate program, in our case, called the Victorian Certificate of Education (VCE). Teachers often say to Year 10 classes, 'This is your preparation for VCE. We will teach you just like VCE.' Surely students only need to hear this a few times before they say, 'Well in that case, I'll wait for VCE to start, when it really counts!'

Running small classes is a financial nightmare, so we discussed the idea of abolishing Year 10 altogether and rolling them all into what we termed the Three Year VCE. Those students wanting to pursue a trade could start their Victorian Certificate of Applied Learning (VCAL) one year early, without wasting yet another year on a largely academically focused conventional Year 10 program which they didn't value. Instead, they could graduate in five years rather than six. Students who did not reach the Year 11 benchmark could remain in the same class but be assessed at a Year 10 academic level. Most beneficially, students could spread their academic load over three rather than two years and either take a broader range of subjects, repeat subjects to get a higher score, or take on a non-assessed elective like Art, Drama, Sport or Music. Students repeating a subject ended up improving their score by an average of 18-20% the second time around; other students appreciated the stress relief of an extra set of study classes or took a non-assessed elective such as Music, Art or Sport pursued just for the pleasure of it.

We were aware of some research that says that students studying a subject at an older age will generally perform better in that subject, however this does not take into account the students' specific circumstances, motivations for formal study and competing interests. As educators, too often we assume we know what is best for a student and make decisions accordingly based on our own world views. Staff at TC were encouraged to still express their opinions and to give advice to students, but we did not preclude students from selecting their own program from the full range of choices available to them. One of the often cited sayings among both students and staff was 'whose education is this?'

Combining Years 10-12 within the one senior program meant that class sizes were larger while simultaneously providing a broader curriculum offering. Once we removed year levels altogether, we saw these financial benefits increase even further along with the pedagogical benefits as 15% of Year 8 aged students and 75% of Year 9 aged students successfully attempted a normally Year 11 VCE subject. Many of our young people ended up with far broader academic programs than would normally be possible as they were able to take their conventional two-year senior program over three, four even five years. By questioning the assumptions of age-based progression we ended up not only with higher levels of engagement, better results, greater levels of student agency but it made financial sense as well. We were able to provide students and staff with some of the best resources and finance some excellent student-led programs at the same operating cost.

NO OR LOW-COST LOCAL PARTNERSHIPS

We became aware of a program where commercial gymnasiums were being established within a small number of independent schools that would service parents before school, students during the day and the wider community after school. We had ample space, but almost non-existent gym facilities. We entered into an arrangement where a gym provider would provide high-quality gymnasium equipment at no cost in return for rent and provide supervised access to the gym at lunchtime. We ended up with a young enthusiastic franchise holder who we then engaged to conduct gym classes throughout the day as a contractor, the cost of which could then be legitimately passed on to parents. It was substantially cheaper than a gym membership, meant that students could improve their fitness, and allowed us to offer another range of electives at a far lower cost than employing a PE teacher. Because the instructor was not teaching, but instead offering a commercial service of instruction, and no one was being displaced, the Union was satisfied. The ownership of the gym eventually passed to our Chaplain who was a fitness fanatic and for years provided not only fitness instruction, but used the time to check up on, monitor and provide incidental counselling with a significant number of our young people in a far less intrusive and natural manner.

The entrepreneurial principal

Future School principals needs to be entrepreneurial in their own outlook, always on the watch for opportunities to improve student learning options within a limited budget.

One example we recently saw was a small school which happened to be located in a thriving and vibrant arts community. Rather than employing Art and Technology teachers on small fractional time allotments, which would be cost prohibitive, instead they operated a 'before school program' taught by local artists that finished at 10am before the official start of school. This not only saved money but ensured students could learn from a wider range of high-quality practising artists without the restrictive nature of teacher registration, and also helped to build stronger links to the community.

Keep your eyes out for services that community members or organisations can provide to supplement the learning program. Many are far more cost-effective than employing teacher staff directly and may have far more contemporary skills.

RESOURCE CENTRE (THE RC)

When I started at TC, I was conscious that although we had a huge amount of building and space there were no areas for students to sit in warmth outside of class time other than the library. It was quite a conventional space with a HUGE number of old books. Apparently, it had been a shared municipal library and whenever a neighbouring library shut down, the old Templestowe College would be given the books. I made the comment that while our old books were lovely and warm during winter, our kids were not. Even though our numbers had declined our library staff had remained constant. We had a full-time teacher librarian and 1.5 library assistants, so the teacher librarian Wayne was redeployed to take on the VCAL program which he took on with gusto. When we looked at the books' borrowing tags, many had not been borrowed in more than ten years. Sally galvanised the library staff and some student volunteers into action, packing up any books that were subject related and sending them for display and storage in the faculty area, keeping our newest editions and enquiring about sending our old books overseas. It turns out that old encyclopedias are not highly prized items overseas and therefore we had two skips of books sent to be pulped. We now had a quite sizeable warm space to begin working with students.

We wanted the students to feel welcome, so we set up a station with two microwaves and an urn with coffee, tea and hot chocolate. Sally would also bring in the occasional cake, tray of chocolate biscuits or box of fruit as treats. It was a very cost-effective cultural intervention. The aim was to communicate to students that we cared about not only their learning but about them personally. We wanted to make school a little more like home. Sally and I went shopping for furniture and bought twelve large microfibre couches. Several staff questioned how long they would last. It really was a sign of the prevailing staff culture that students cannot be trusted so we should be very cautious about giving them anything of value. Those couches were used relentlessly every single day, shifted by students countless times as the RC space was reconfigured for various uses. Occasionally a nest of rats needed to be decamped and yet they survived and remained relatively presentable for five years.

Student amenities – a measure of how much you care

We have seen the equivalent of a Resource Centre established in many schools always with considerable success.

Are there places in your school for all students to sit in relative comfort during bad weather?

Are the facilities at least the equivalent quality to those for staff?

What does this say about our world view about the relative importance and worth of young people?

The Resource Centre

We had a horrible piece of apparatus that I felt looked like the wings of a Star Wars TIE Fighter near the exit door of the Resource Centre. As you walked through on exit, it made an unpleasant clicking noise that I interpreted to mean, 'I think you may be stealing a book and I'm just checking'. I asked the librarians if our students stealing books was really our biggest issue. We could hardly get them to engage with books at all! We did a calculation with the library staff checking how long it took to cover the book, insert the security tag and put it on the borrowing system. Once staff time was taken into account, it equated to far more than the cost of the book. Essentially if the book was not stolen within the first twelve months we would be ahead. So from that point on students could come, take an uncovered uncatalogued book and return it once they were finished with it. Yes, occasionally we did have parents return multiple books stamped with the TC logo, but on the whole the honour system worked exceptionally well. I would question how many students look up a library catalogue rather than selecting a book based on active promotion by being visible. We made the promise to students that if they wanted a book, we would order it and they could be the first to borrow it. We also came across an unexpected benefit in terms of parents bringing in tubs of barely used books from home and adding them to our shelves and later created our mobile library boxes that students constructed and were strategically installed around the school.

We did some investigation and found that under the Employment Award a senior educational support staff member could supervise up to around 100 students provided they had ready access to backup support and were not delivering the curriculum. Led by an enthusiastic, highly relational, tertiary qualified support staff member in the new role of 'RC Manager', the Resource Centre became the place where students went when there was not a classroom teacher.

Leaders should carefully consider what value students really obtain from the huge amount of money spent on casual relief teachers. Teachers were required to not only leave work when they were away, but to ensure that emergency extras were left in case they had a migraine and were not in a position to leave work. Not only did this cut an enormous amount from the budget but it also significantly reduced the follow-up on behavioural incidents that inevitably result from students interacting with adults charged with 'getting the work done' with whom they don't have an existing relationship.

In an effort to increase our attractiveness to parents we opened the Resource Centre from 7am to after 5pm so that parents could use the school for semi-supervised before and after school care. We would say that it was the students' school and they could stay until we left which was often 7pm. When we had a college council meeting, it was not uncommon to have international students staying back working and socialising until 10pm. I have to say that Sally and I became a virtual mother and father to around twenty-five students across a range of ages during this time who became almost like extended family to each other. We brought up some table-tennis tables from the PE department and board games from the library cupboards and watched the students play games with each other and then assist each other with school work. In addition, we offered after-school tutoring from Monday to Thursday, initially by adult staff but in later years by trained, paid student tutors. These were all little extras not offered by other neighbouring schools and made the TC option just that little bit more attractive.

The Resource Centre quickly became known as somewhere warm, comfortable and playful and there were always adults and older students around to help students solve problems. We soon moved our IT facilities to the RC where students ran an IT help desk. Throughout my eight years at TC, the Resource Centre kept evolving, was renovated twice but always remained the beating heart of the school.

The power of a name

Knowing a person's name is a powerful acknowledgement of their worth as a person. For leaders in schools, it should certainly extend beyond the brightest and the notorious. Personally, I think it is not unrealistic for classroom teachers to know each and every young person they teach by name within four weeks. As a young teacher I was impressed that my first Headmaster, Rick Tudor, could recognise a student by the back of their head in assembly and literally knew every student in the school population of 1300 and something about them and the names of many of their parents. While his memory for names was naturally strong, which mine is certainly not, he once told me that each morning as he ate his breakfast he would flick through the printed school photographs and reinforce those names he was struggling with. I used this technique since it was passed on to me and can generally manage around 700 student names comfortably. Interestingly as the school population goes past that, my recall drops quite quickly to around 350, because unless you are using students' names regularly and with confidence the names of those students who you know less well can become confused in your mind, so you stop using the name of any student you are unsure of.

Remembering names comes easier to some people than others, but is something that all educators should actively work on. It sounds tacky and perhaps politically incorrect, but one trick I have tried is to draw on the photographs, adding some detail that might help me access the name. A shoe for Schumann, an anvil for Smith, a medal for Nguyen. My own capacity to remember names has perhaps influenced my belief that the ideal size for a school, either primary/secondary or Preparatory to Year 12, should be around 650 students.

How reliably can you recall students' names? Is this a technique that could benefit you?

NO HOMEWORK BUT HOME-LEARNING

As a fan of American educational author and paradigm challenger, Alfie Kohn, I was aware of the sizeable amount of research that said that homework offered little in terms of academic gain before Year 10. These findings have been repeated numerous times in international and national research. It puzzled me then as it does now as to why educators continue to make work for themselves and students when the evidence around the benefits are so flimsy. There are also huge potential costs in terms of student engagement, academic self-perception, creating conflict within families. I recall my younger daughter's experience of homework. A keen self-driven student of neuroscience and anatomy, she came home one day and told us with delight that the class would be studying the brain. Two days later she burst through the door exclaiming, 'I hate the brain!' Her natural love for the topic had been destroyed by a tedious and unimaginative homework assignment.

I once approached a local primary school principal who was held in very high esteem for the school's excellent NAPLAN results, asking why she enforced a strict homework regime for students and staff. I asked if she was aware of the research. 'Oh yes,' she said. I persisted, 'You're aware that the research says that it makes no difference in primary school and almost no difference up until Year 10?' 'Yes, I am,' she said, 'and I believe it, but my Asian parents generally don't!'

Australian young people spend more time in class than anyone, anywhere.

Australians already spend the equivalent of three years more compulsory time in class than any other OECD country besides Denmark, and five years longer than the impressive Finnish education system. Having more learning time is not the answer, having students more engaged is the answer. My good friend Professor Pasi Sahlberg has been pointing this out for many years now. How is it that this fact does not raise questions of how we use class time and why we persist with the nonsense of homework?

Reference: Pasi Sahlberg Finnish Lessons 3.0

Total number of compulsory instruction hours in primary and lower secondary schools

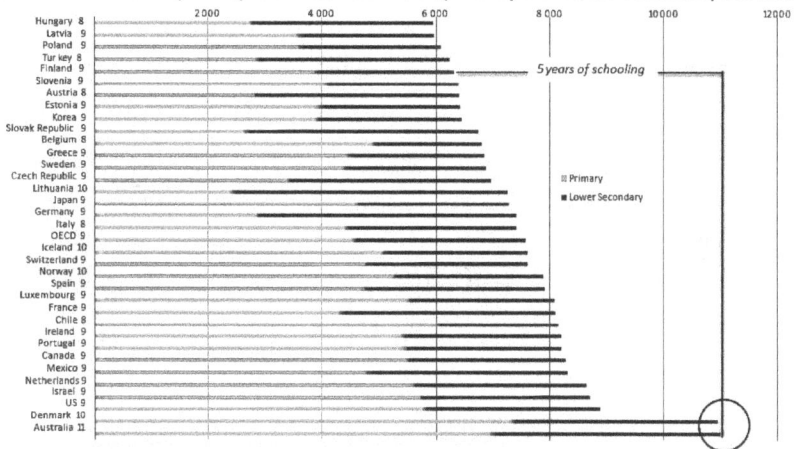

At TC, we made it clear that we would follow the research and while we would not prescribe boring homework, we did encourage families to undertake Home-Learning. I explained my belief to the staff that if the learning task was so important, then it should be done in class with appropriate support and guidance. 'What's done in class, must be enough to pass' became another TC mantra. Staff had to ensure that any assignment was given enough time that if a student applied themselves reasonably conscientiously in class time, then they should be able to achieve a passing grade without any homework. We did explain to students and their families that based on their personal plan for the future and whether it required university study, that some of them would need to work beyond normal class hours, but that this would be their choice. Of course students can continue to learn and advance their understanding of concepts outside class, but it really does rely on a positive and engaged mindset.

Here is an extract from the information in our student diary:

Home-Learning is open to students in non-VCE subjects. This policy is based on research and involves parents in the development and monitoring of your Individual Learning Program. This practice relies on the partnership between you, your parent/guardians and the College.

Key Points from the Policy include:

At Year 7-9 level our recommendation is for students to complete a minimum of ten hours of quality self-directed Home-Learning over the week. Each student's Home-Learning Plan will be different based on the student's areas of interest, level of skill development and their individual plans and ambitions.

Tasks may include:

· Clubs, Scouts, youth group
· Completing real jobs & real tasks for others

- Dance, Martial arts or other physical activities
- Discussing ideas & values & current events
- Discussion of work completed at school
- Exercise
- Extension ideas
- Finishing off learning tasks started at school
- Hobbies
- Listening to audio books
- Music practice
- Personalised learning tasks negotiated with staff
- Planning for the next lesson
- Preparing revision & study notes
- Reading, reading & more reading
- Rehearsing presentations
- Shopping & cooking a meal
- Spelling & grammar revision
- Sports training
- Test preparation
- Timetables & basic mental maths revision
- Touch typing
- Watching documentaries
- Working on the student ePortfolio
- Working on student's own Home-Learning projects.

Home-Learning Projects

Students are encouraged to design and prepare their own Home-Learning Project in an area of their interest. At the student's discretion this project can be presented to a panel comprising friends, parents, teachers, even outside experts in the particular field to receive feedback and encouragement.

It is the student's responsibility to:

- Plan their Home-Learning activities to maximise their learning given their own plan and goals
- Set tasks that are challenging and motivating
- Keep an honest and accurate record of their activities
- Ensure a balance between Home-Learning activities
- Discuss their Home-Learning with their parents/guardian and their learning mentor.

It is the parent/guardian's responsibility to:

- Negotiate and regularly review the Home-Learning plan with their son/daughter
- Assist the young person to evaluate the balance between various activities given their plans and goals
- Encourage and support the young person to develop their own Home-Learning projects
- Assist the student to monitor and assess their own Home-Learning performance
- Verify that the Weekly Home Learning Log is correct each week and give constructive feedback.
- Contact the learning mentor if the process is not working effectively.

It is the learning mentor's responsibility to:

- Talk with the student about their Home-Learning plan and their progress
- Evaluate the balance between various activities in regard to helping the student achieve their plans and goals
- Encourage and support the student to develop their own Home-Learning assignments

- Refer any questions or concerns that are not able to be resolved to the student's Head of House or Classroom Teachers or other staff member as appropriate.

This was a great initiative, reflecting that learning not only takes place within school hours and within the classroom but everywhere during waking hours. It put the responsibility for learning and progress with the student, with the parents and mentor in support roles. It enabled students to focus on what they wanted to learn and get recognition for it by the school. Many parents expressed a huge relief at the concept of Home-Learning, pleased that they no longer needed to be the police officer at home and they reported far more harmonious family lives. They also appreciated being provided with the actual research, rather than the common expectation that 'homework is good for students'. The only problem was – it didn't work for all that many families.

Home-Learning was great in theory but many of our families did not have the determination, or perhaps given the busyness of modern life, the time to follow this through effectively. The staff were working so hard to stay on top of all the new changes at the school, that mentors rarely followed up with the monitoring and encouragement. I do believe that many families supported Home-Learning, but in a more organic incidental way reminiscent of most home schooling. On several occasions the Leadership Group tried to re-energise it, but I can't really claim the documentation of the process was ever a true success. Ten years on, I still believe in the concept, but staff would need to have significantly more time if they were to support Home-Learning beyond a mere compliance role. I include this tale to illustrate that not everything we tried worked. Given the ineffectiveness of traditional homework, I don't believe that any students were harmed by this process; indeed Home-Learning allowed them to validate and feel positive about many of the excellent learning activities students were already doing as individuals or with their families.

ONE-TO-ONE LAPTOP PROGRAM

The Federal Government at the time was keen to see the use of laptops expand. They had a program in government schools where they would supply one laptop between two students. As luck would have it, they took the numbers on the previous year's census and with our numbers dropping from 423 to 284, less the forty international students all of whom bought their own computer, we only had to buy thirty-two computers to give **every** student a machine. We looked at the theory that was around at the time about how to successfully launch a one-to-one laptop program and found something called 'The 21 steps to 1:1 laptop integration', which talked about preparing the staff, students and the community by leading them through twenty-one detailed steps that would ensure a successful roll-out and implementation. We jumped straight to step twenty-one. We bought and distributed the machines and then began the race to make the best use of them. Providing each student with a machine on a three-year leasing program where the families paid a third of the cost of the machine each year would mean that the program could become sustainable even when the government subsidy was dropped. With that we were the only state school in our area and one of only three state schools in Victoria at the time to be 1:1.

Exploring the grey space

It was 'somewhat unclear' whether we were permitted to pass on this cost to parents. My feeling was that it was not explicitly prohibited, no staff member was profiting in any way, and there was no statement explaining how schools could continue to fund it when the subsidy finished. Clearly it was a political vote grab that we see from time to time without a well-thought out idea of how it would continue to be funded. Our parents and students were simply delighted to all have their own machine, that they could also take home at a vastly reduced price, rather than sharing a machine between two that could not be taken home. It is one of those marginal calls that you are sometimes forced to make as a principal where we stand to gain nothing personally but where we take on the risk of a slap over the knuckles or worse for making decisions in the best interest of our students.

You do need to be careful how often you take these risks, and to be clear, fraud or embezzlement are bridges that should <u>never</u> be crossed, but from time to time there is a grey space that can be exploited for the benefits of young people.

LEADERSHIP TEAM MEMBERSHIP EXTENDED TO INCLUDE STUDENT VOLUNTEERS

I thought 'what better way to capture student opinion than to expand the composition of the Leadership Team to include student members?' Fortunately, there were several students keen to be involved. We thought that in order to ensure they could make more informed decisions, we would give them an induction course that included staffing, school budgeting, learning theory, timetabling and an explanation of some of the key department regulations. To our surprise as we conducted these sessions over a number of weeks in parallel to running the new larger Leadership Group, their contributions actually decreased!

When we explored this with the students, we found that rather than giving them greater confidence they were discovering more and more ways that they could be wrong or be seen as making a silly suggestion. Rather than get our desired student input, we were actually training up very junior and inexperienced school leaders.

A quick pivot saw us abandon these preparation classes and forsake continuity for swapping these groups of students over every ten weeks. We got what we wanted, raw student input and reactions, and simultaneously a greater number of students had the opportunity of experiencing the genuine behind-the-scenes organisation of the school.

Students on Staff Selection Panels

In August 2011 we extended the involvement of students to include sitting on staff selection panels. From a legal perspective the student panel role is purely advisory, and we made the argument it was no different to having prospective staff teach a demonstration lesson, or for students to take a tour of the school, and then ask for the students' feedback.

We adapted the Department's own Merit and Equity training package and delivered it to any student who wished to be part of the selection pool. We ended up training approximately thirty students at a time, where the students learnt firsthand about open and closed questioning, the type of information that could be sought to make a judgement and workshopped their own scenario questions.

The student panels would eventually be led by a more experienced student who had previously sat on a number of panels and knew the procedure. They would set up the room, ensure there was fresh water and glasses, that the questions were prepared and allocated beforehand. They would then collect the prospective staff member, show them into the room, introduce the student panel members, ask them a few warm-up questions and then get down to business. At the end of the interview, they would thank the interviewee for their time, explain the next stage of the process and then bring them across to the staff panel. Prospective staff were always told in advance that they would be interviewed by an additional student panel. We knew if they were put off by this, then they would not be a great fit for TC. Almost without exception the feedback we received from both successful and unsuccessful candidates was glowing and the feedback that the adult panel received from students was invaluable in guiding our deliberations.

What were we looking for? We were not looking for the student panels' opinion as to the applicants' academic suitability and for privacy reasons did not give the students access to the interviewees' applications. What we did want was their impression of how they would fit with the burgeoning TC culture. Did they treat the students as children, as equals or as superiors? We regularly had all three responses. Having shared this process with many visitors to TC, I am often asked what kind of relationship the students were look- ing for, and did they ever become over familiar once the successful candidate started in their role? My impression is that the students wanted to be treated respectfully as equals, with an understanding that it was their learning and they wanted the staff member to allow them to take responsibility for it. They did want someone with great subject knowledge and someone who had passion and would inspire them. I cannot recall any staff member mentioning that a student had taken advantage of starting the power balance in this way, but to be honest I would not really care if they did. Any such indiscretion would have provided the opportunity for a 'teachable moment' for the staff member to talk about respectful relationships and I have faith that the vast majority could handle this sensibly, sensitively and without making a big deal of it.

'WHAT'S YOUR PLAN?'

'What's your plan?' became a central part of the TC language. It was asked on enrolment, at subject selection, when asking a student about their less than desirable behaviour and as they graduated. Everything traced back to the student's plan for the future, so that we could look at any decisions they were currently making and together check for alignment. It was also a far less confrontational way of starting a conversation with students and demonstrated that our primary interest was not their uniform, but rather whether they were on track with their own plan. The conversation might eventually swing around to their uniform non-compliance for example but not always. The student inevitably knew what the indiscretion was that had captured the staff member's attention in the first instance and would remedy it, or at worst the staff member might end with, 'I hate to end such a great conversation talking with you about uniform. Can you fix that up, please?' These were not superficial conversations and it was a joy to listen to students unpack and modify their plans over time. Sometimes it elicited a response of 'I really don't know.' This then presented an opportunity to get them back on a track that they were committed to, even if just for the short term.

Naturally students will change their minds over time and they may only have a general idea of their interest areas. 'I want to pursue something to do with ....' was certainly a very acceptable answer.

A follow-up question that I would ask today is, 'And what are you doing that moves you towards that plan now?' Too much about school is endlessly preparing for the future. Young people need to be supported to live life here and now, so they can make significant contributions to their broader community and doing things that start moving them closer to their goals. They also need to be reassured that to reassess and change goals is a very natural thing to do.

THE WORST – BEST YEAR OF THEIR LIVES

Together Sally and I thought that if the school was going to close, we would make it the best year of the students' lives. We encouraged each class to run at least one excursion and take their learning to the community. We even ran movie nights and sleepovers at the school, took part in the Rock Eisteddfod, took students swimming with the dolphins, surfing, offered free excursions, ran myriad camps and offered heavily subsidised evening excursions to the theatre to expose students to opportunities they would not normally experience.

While many students enjoyed some of these activities, many remained uncommitted. Some would say they were attending and simply not turn up on the evening with the flimsiest of excuses the next day. I must confess, I started to feel angry and a little resentful. Didn't they know how hard we were trying to give them great educational experiences? Then it dawned on me… yet again 'we' were the ones orchestrating these experiences. They had no buy-in. Many of our students came from well-off families and with parents who regularly did 'too much' for their children. We were just more adults, providing yet more experiences that they could choose from. So a quick pivot, and an announcement was made. From the start of next year, instead of doing everything, we would be doing nothing! A stunned silence from the whole school assembly. Unless students chose to do it! 'They' could do almost anything, but 'they' had to organise it.

Who is doing all the work?

How much are you doing for your students? Do you ever feel resentful when they don't react with quite the enthusiasm you had hoped for? Perhaps, just perhaps, they don't have the buy-in, simply because YOU have already paid the bill. Could it be you have over-invested, thus leaving little room for them to take control?

Chapter Six

GETTING STAFF ON BOARD

INITIAL STAFF RESPONSE

Many people have asked me what the early response was by staff to the dramatic and rapid changes they were being asked to make. The honest response was 'mixed'. After a period of almost twelve months of uncertainty about the direction of the College with an acting principal in place, people finally had a clear direction and I feel that I presented as someone who was determined to achieve it, in spite of my internal uncertainty and angst. I knew the theory from my military leadership training of the significantly increased likelihood of success of having a clear plan, enthusiastically communicated and quickly executed.

STAFF QUESTIONS

In those early days the proposed innovations were mainly my ideas, but most certainly augmented and refined for our context by the leadership group, particularly Assistant Principal Sally and a small group of keen and committed staff at all levels. While I am a strong believer in the wisdom of the crowd and benefits of collaboration, those first few years at TC were, in reality, a benevolent dictatorship. We would hold regular staff meetings where I would outline my proposed direction and attempt to explain the way I saw education changing at Templestowe College. These meetings were not always pleasant and some were quite hostile. I was new, I was asking them not only to change significantly but change quickly. I now realise they were most likely afraid. Afraid that they could not adapt quickly enough. Afraid of not being seen as the authority in the classroom. Afraid that under this new system they might not be regarded as a 'good teacher' and afraid that in spite of their best efforts it still might not be enough to turn the school around before it was closed.

Taking questions, and there were lots of them at staff meetings, was very challenging in those early years… and in some of the later years too. While I very much respected the group of colleagues that I worked with, I would not say that even at the end of my time at TC that we were a highly cohesive team and certainly not of one mind. This has caused me to question and reflect on my leadership approach and I have certainly seen many principals assemble more unified teams. I think that because TC was so diverse, so different, that we attracted creative, more free-thinking staff. The one thing that united us was that we, almost to an individual, put the students first. We all wanted what was in their best interests. We just had different ideas about what was best for them and how to support them to achieve this. On reflection, perhaps such diversity of opinions, sometimes expressed in heated debate was a good sign, where people felt safe to express their true thoughts. It did not always feel positive at the time, and I think this is worthwhile passing on to anyone leading staff in a troubled school and planning a rapid reform agenda.

One approach I learnt in those first few years was handling staff questions about a potential new change. By the time I presented a new idea to staff I had thought through most of the obvious implications. That was because while staff rightly concentrated primarily on their teaching or fulfilling their roles, my mind was almost constantly turning over ways to improve the school. When staff would ask questions, I would always have an answer, well at least to most things. I DID want and need the staff questions as it helped me work through in my mind if I had missed anything or where I needed to explain aspects of the plan in more detail. I received some excellent advice from an older and wiser staff member who said, 'You don't need to show you know the answer to every question. Just look contemplative and take a few more questions on notice.' It was sage advice and encouraged far more meaningful discussions at staff meetings.

I did not always consult staff as a group *prior* to presenting the idea to the community, indeed some of the biggest ideas were presented first to an assembly of the whole school. The reality was that I did not want certain influential staff to have the opportunity to challenge and tear down an idea before it had a chance to be run past the students. Most changes were a redistribution of power in favour of young people, giving them more rights and autonomy. Had staff expressed sufficient concern, it would have been difficult for me to continue to run the idea past the students. When challenged by the Union representatives about the need for consultation, which for the purposes of our work agreement was defined as…

Consultation is providing the individual, or other relevant persons, with a bona fide opportunity to influence the decision maker… Consultation is not joint decision-making or even a negative or frustrating barrier to the prerogative of management to make decisions. Consultation allows the decision-making process to be informed, particularly as it may affect the employment prospects of individuals.

My response was, 'But you were all there, it was presented for consultation to the students and staff alike and as part of our one-person policy, it would be wrong to privilege one section of the community over another.' After the assembly, students would often then move to Mentor Groups for discussion where staff and students had the opportunity to submit questions, opinions or suggestions. Once staff had seen a positive reaction from students to the majority of proposals, whose satisfaction we all knew was the key to our survival, it was harder for them to oppose an idea.

At another staff meeting I expressed that rather than thinking of me being the new one at the school, it would be easier for the staff to imagine that THEY were the ones at a new school. I explained that if we couldn't turn this school around and the staff did end up at a new school, they would not be saying, 'That's not how we did things at Templestowe.' Instead they would say, 'Wow, that's interesting, I wonder how that works,' and then give the new practice a try. That was all I was asking. That they suspend their disbelief and give these new ideas and ways of operating a try before condemning the idea.

Grow the school rather than pruning dead wood

Many new principals of troubled schools receive advice to focus their initial attention on 'cleaning out underperforming staff'. In well-established, stable schools focusing attention on a few underperforming staff can be a legitimate strategy. However, coming into a small and struggling school, this approach might not make the best sense. Working to remove underperforming staff is incredibly time-consuming, emotionally draining and does not make for building an optimistic and trusting staff climate. With the exception of allowing the actions of staff who are harming students in any way to go unchecked, my advice would be to 'work with who you have' and try and grow the school as quickly as possible. As the school grows each new staff member employed allows you to inject new capacity, enthusiasm and is usually someone more aligned to your way of thinking, while simultaneously diluting the impact of less desirable cultural norms. A small school can double in size and even with natural attrition you can soon find yourself having appointed more than half the staff. This is a far more positive and effective way of achieving significant cultural change.

STAFF MEETINGS

I must confess that staff meetings were not events that I looked forward to, particularly in those early days. Staff were nervous, many were trying to actively get work elsewhere and I suspect some were scared that I would ask more of them than they could deliver.

I genuinely wanted staff buy-in, but I also felt an incredible pressure to keep the school moving forwards. I recall a staff member saying in an open meeting, 'You seem to care more about the students than you do about us!' I was momentarily dumbstruck. I then said, 'That's right. And I only want to work with other professionals who think the same.' I then went on to explain that as adults we had choices. We could stay or go, but many of our students did not have those choices.

I think I made a point that day. I certainly explained my world view in relation to putting students' needs first. But, today, with my current understanding, I think I was wrong. It is not a binary situation where you have to put the needs of one group above those of another. It is far more complex than that. My current belief is that you are best treating all people with compassion and respect and to take the needs of each individual as well as the needs of the school into account. This is not to say that I have 'softened', indeed I think I would have even higher expectations of staff and students were I in the same position again. I would, however, take more time to outline my thinking, make myself more available for discussion and be more open to the suggestions of others. Back then I was very conscious of not having the staff meetings extend beyond the time allocated in the agreement and as a result, sometimes I rushed the process. My current stance would still be to conclude business within the set time but to stay behind to talk with those who wanted to continue the discussion and be available during the next day at lunchtime. My learning is that key decisions cannot be rushed, yet can still be made in a timely manner and with everyone feeling heard and respected.

I am also in favour of any meeting protocols that allow greater representation, so that ALL people have the opportunity to speak and be heard. There is always a risk that the same few, often oppositional, voices are heard which can be as equally damaging as a leader dominating too much of the discussion. One practice I did not appreciate was one person self-nominating as 'the spokesperson' or the 'voice of the people'. I encouraged each person to express their views but not to claim to represent the power of unidentified others. I would approach anyone who claimed the role of spokesperson and say I am happy with you being the spokesperson as long as you have a list of names and signatures of those you represent. Otherwise, put your comments forward as your own opinion, and I will take your comments as being as important as my own or anyone else's in the school. I really did want genuine debate and discussion, but I did not want to encourage staff rallying support for their cause in the corridors and staffrooms as though sheer numbers alone added weight to their argument.

NOT WHITE ANTS... WHITE POINTERS!

Early on there were a few staff who were not so much white-anting my moves at innovation, so much as white-pointering. They were outspoken and had quite a degree of power to influence the tone of meetings and the overall mood of the staff. I asked to see each one individually, with a support person present and said, 'Our situation is essentially a marriage of inconvenience. Neither one of us chose the other. You don't want me here and to be frank, I don't really want you here either. But you can't get out and I understand you're concerned, but if you bring this school down I am pretty confident your colleagues are not going to thank you for it. We have one shot at this and it has to work so this is the deal I am prepared to offer. As long as you don't harm the students, I will leave you alone for three years. But if you choose not to take this offer, I have been assured by HR that they will bring the full weight of the Department down upon you. I will leave it for you to consider.'

To their great credit, after three years two staff were well and truly on board with the new model and had taken on leadership positions while one had chosen to leave. These conversations were very difficult for me and essentially, I was bluffing, as I had not discussed the situation with anyone at the Department.

MANAGING STAFF CLAIMS OF OVERWORK

At TC in those early years, I did pile on several new changes in addition to the work teachers and support staff were currently undertaking. My honest impression now as it was then, was that staff had become complacent and in spite of earnest intent had lost touch with how hard educational professionals were working in other schools. I am not sure this comment will win me a lot of favour with my former colleagues. It is not that they were not filling their hours, indeed many were working well beyond the thirty-eight hours required of them, but they were doing what they *liked* to do or thought was most valuable rather than working in any coordinated way in the best interests of young people.

This again sounds harsh, but when staff complained of overwork, I would emphasise that we (the leadership team) only wanted to be able to direct the thirty-eight hours that they signed up for. If they felt they were doing more than this allocation, I invited them to keep a work diary explaining when and on what they were working. I offered to sit down with them and remove those tasks I believed were less valuable to the school and achieving our vision. I only had two staff take me up on this offer. Both had numerous significant extra-curricular activities they were contributing to. So while they were indeed doing more than their thirty-eight hours, with much of their preparation time, lunchtimes, afterschool and even weekends spent on things *they* liked to do. When I said that they should drop some of these activities their comment was 'But I really like doing that bit of my job.' My comment was that this was not really part of their job, but it was rather their hobby and while I would be delighted if they continued, it was their choice to do so.

I commented at a staff meeting that almost all of us contribute more than thirty-eight hours a week to the school on a regular basis. That is because education is a passion for us and we love to support young people. My directive is give beyond your thirty-eight hours when you want to give and feel up to the task, pull back when you don't. Feeling obligated to give beyond what is mandated breeds resentment and to be honest giving so much can also take away learning opportunities from young people in terms of them stepping up and taking greater responsibility for their education, particularly in co-curricular activities.

Making room for change

Change is time intensive and cognitively more demanding. Doing anything for the first time or until it becomes habitual takes longer and also requires more concentration and cognitive load. When you are undertaking a significant transformation agenda in your school this will take up some of the cognitive load of staff. You do need to make room for this additional load by taking some things away BEFORE introducing your latest new idea. This will certainly get a better reception and have a greater chance of succeeding than piling on another new thing. I acknowledge that this is something that I learnt later in TC's change process.

UNION INVOLVEMENT

In terms of the Unions, I always adopted a very open stance. In Victorian state schools there is an agreement that union officials must ask permission of the principal before coming on site and understandably must not disrupt teachers or staff from their duties. I met with the Union Representatives early in my first term and gave them open access to the site at any time and said that we both had a similar goal for the staff at Templestowe not to lose their jobs. While the majority of staff would have been placed in other schools, if the school did close, clearly it would cause a lot of stress for Union members. I acknowledged my colours as being the son of a trade union organiser and all I asked was that if they had an issue that they would come and talk so that we could work things out amicably as early as possible. In my eight years at TC, we did not have one Union dispute.

Do Unions add or detract when turning around a troubled school?

Personally, I believe in the need for unions, as I have seen some teaching and support staff treated very, very unfairly which was able to be pushed through by leaders because staff did not have any bargaining power, significant legal or external support. I have, however, seen some jurisdictions where in an attempt to retain power, Union activity has extended their influence into slowing down or totally thwarting educational leaders' efforts to innovate. Like most situations this is complex, but with transparency and an acknowledged desire to ensure that all people's interests are advanced, those of both students AND staff, most situations should be able to be successfully negotiated.

Chapter Seven

A MORE FLEXIBLE STRUCTURE

HOUSE AND MENTOR SYSTEM

I have always been a strong believer in vertical (multi-age) wellbeing structures, often associated with a House system. My idea is that where you have relatively stable staffing, the same capable and caring adults can work with students from the start of their schooling journey to the end, ideally with relationships with both the student and their family continuing to deepen and be enriched over time. It also means that a House can develop its own unique culture and gives greater purpose to the sports days that occur regularly in most school calendars.

As a sign of our unwavering confidence that the school would increase to our planned size of 650 students, which represented one hundred students per year level of four full classes, and fifty international students on top of that, we presented our new idea. It seemed illogical to wait so instead we wanted to divide the existing four Houses that had no real function other than sport and reallocate the Heads of Year Level. Given that numbers had just fallen under three hundred, this did seem a little audacious, even naïve and a number of staff passed cynical comments, but the Leadership Group pressed on.

In negotiating this change with the SRC, we agreed that no one should feel obligated to change House but instead be invited to do so. We sold the idea that it would enable students to be part of building a new House culture from the ground up, to forever be a part of TC history as the co-founders of the two new Houses. Some moved for this reason, some because they had already developed a less than positive relationship with their Head of House and wanted a new start and some offered to move if they could be assured a move that would unite their friendship group. It meant that no one was forced to move and we could use students who would be new to the school next year to correct the slight imbalance in the numbers. Naturally students were consulted on whether we would select two new names that built upon the existing set of names based on southern sky constellations, Phoenix, Aquilla, Dorado and Centaur, or rename all the houses on another basis. Student suggestions included famous Australians, famous scientists or Indigenous place names. In the end students voted to keep and build upon the existing names based on southern sky constellations and so two new Houses, Orion and Pegasus, were born.

In most schools each House is then divided up further into Mentor Groups or Home Groups which usually cross year level, but I have seen Houses divided up by year level as well. Many people are keen on this model and see it as the best of both worlds. A teacher can become more of a specialist in a particular developmental level and for the Head of House it really does become like a school within a school.

In reflecting on my past experience across three schools which had vertical house systems, I observed that it was usually possible to get capable and committed Heads of House but the quality of those undertaking Mentor roles was highly variable. At worst some staff saw the role of Mentor as an imposition and an administrative duty rather than a pastoral one. The other issue was that Mentor Groups were often reformed each year to balance numbers, with little regard given to continuity of care. My question was, what if students could select their own Mentor from *any* adult in the school? So began a move to new hybrid model seeking to get the best from the House system and give the students a real and broad choice about who looked out for them.

To ensure that the pool of potential Mentors was large and to keep groups small we would ask all staff members, teaching or support, to be a Mentor. There was some disquiet about non-teaching staff taking up wellbeing roles with students and questions were raised about the legalities of supervision and the ability of 'non-teachers' to give advice on academic matters. I have always found quite conservative views around the presumed capacity of non-teachers to fulfil these functions and an almost complete disregard for the idea that support staff might have anything at all to offer when it comes to students. My experience has shown me that it really does come down to the nature of the individual. I have observed some excellent support staff, even senior students, who are already skilled 'teachers' and many qualified 'teachers' who lack the basics in terms of care and guidance of young people. These concerns were eventually solved by asking each support staff member to select a teaching staff member who they worked well with to co-locate their groups with. For the sake of transparency, I will disclose that while many support staff were very keen to be involved and saw it as a huge opportunity, some were not so keen or legitimately concerned about the extra work on top of their existing roles. I did take quite a firm stand on this by saying if they could not see themselves as primarily a supporter of the learning and development of young people then they really were out of step with the future directions of the school. From the maintenance person to the lab tech, all our support staff eventually got on board and I would suggest almost all found the experience worthwhile.

One of my fears was that that half the students would select the young energetic English teacher and the other half the vivacious Physical Education teacher. Would only these people's groups be fully allocated and the rest of the staff left with no one? Who would select the gnarly old Woodwork teacher? To reduce this possibility, we asked students to nominate their top five Mentor preferences and also promised that they would have at least one of their five nominated friends. When the slips came in it was amazing to see the spread of first preferences across the staff. No student received lower than their second preference and all had at least one close friend but usually more. We gave the staff the opportunity to decline to take on any student they felt was not a positive match or the relationship with parents was already compromised. The strength of this process was the level of personal connection each student had to their Mentor, which was almost always reciprocated by the Mentor to the student and their family, knowing they had been 'chosen'. The role of the Mentor was purely learning, wellbeing and an advocacy function, leaving all the disciplinary issues to the Head of House. Because the Mentors were not in any way subordinate to the Heads of House (I was a Mentor myself for a few years) they could advocate strongly for fairness on behalf of their mentees and not just accept the 'swift justice' that overworked Heads of House can so often mete out. Mentors acted proactively when they saw the need and were quite ready to voice their concern when they observed inconsistency. This was one of the key successes of building student and parent relationships and connectedness to the school in these early years. I still regret that in later years I agreed to drop this model for the sake of 'efficiency'.

In later years, at the urging of Heads of House who found tracking down Mentors across a larger school population increasingly difficult, we did move to aligning Mentors with Houses to limit the number of Mentors the Head of House had to interact with. The students still had a choice of Learning Mentor but only within their House, or they could choose to change House if they really wanted a particular Learning Mentor. The danger with this later revision is that Heads of House can be strong personalities who often then take over some of the Mentors' role and reduced the Mentors' role as independent advocate and support person for the student. If I were advising on this matter, I believe the optimum to be that students select their own Learning Mentor with the opportunity to transfer as needed. We did find that some students valued being in a Mentor Group with a close friend, rather than who their Learning Mentor was. Another extension on this idea is to allow senior students to also act as Learning Mentors with appropriate training and support.

A proposed alternative to teacher training

Having a teaching qualification does not in itself mean you have the skills or personal attributes to be an adequate teacher. It is almost impossible to fail a trainee teacher, provided they pay their university fees and hand their assignments in on time. There is far too little counselling of people who are clearly unsuitable for the teaching profession in the first few years of teacher training and there is considerable pressure to pass prospective teachers during their teaching rounds.

My belief is that schools should be given the option to hire who they want, and if the staff member proves to be capable, they can undertake their formal training as an integrated part of their work in schools. There would be an incentive for the school to ensure the training was practical and thorough, and the provisionally registered teacher could cover the appropriate academic learning through assignments completed by online asynchronous education.

The current system where a prospective teacher has to effectively give up work or work part-time and therefore complete their teacher training over double the time places an unnecessary financial burden on many people who would otherwise make for exceptional teachers. We would end up with far greater diversity, as well as far fewer poor souls who have undertaken three to four years of study in largely a university-based setting only to find that they are actually unsuited to or simply don't like a real school environment.

LEARNING STREAMS

As planning took place for the second year's intake of fifty-six young people, we were conscious that we had students with quite different needs and focuses. Some students were quite academically able and hugely creative. Others were well enmeshed in the social aspects of adolescence and thrived in situations where they were able to work together and many had a preference for a more verbal/auditory learning style which we termed the Collaborative Learning class. Another group, primarily but not exclusively boys, were in need of more direct instruction and were generally more kinaesthetic, hands-on orientated learners.

We undertook some online testing with the students to determine their preferred learning styles called a VARK assessment, looking at whether students have strengths in visual, auditory, reading or kinaesthetic learning. Current research suggests that there is no academic benefit to be gained by dividing students on the basis of such preferences, but for us it achieved a number of huge benefits. Firstly, it enabled us to have a Direct Instruction class to support students with lower literacy and numeracy levels and teaching them with shorter bursts of direct instruction, supplemented and reinforced with more hands-on tasks. This group also happened to have more boys in it which also helped to bring about a gender balance within the other two classes. We were quite concerned because the incoming cohort were more than two thirds boys and we felt that without this intervention the imbalance of boisterous boys would not provide a positive environment for girls to thrive.

Why are there more boys in alternative education settings?

It is not uncommon to find that schools with a more alternative academic program tend to have significantly more boys enrolled. I attribute this difference to a schooling system that seems to have a greater natural tolerance for girls who are generally less likely to act out. This is not ideal as it does see girls tend to stick with unsuitable schooling environments for longer periods, while parents of disengaged boys tend to move them more readily in response to disciplinary action.

Placement into these classes was always negotiated with the student and their family, and if the student and their parent insisted on being in a particular class then that was the outcome. After all, we wanted students to stay so why would we actively disagree with parents who wanted a particular outcome? Our experience was that most students and parents agreed wholeheartedly with the assessment and were keen to try out a type of learning that was designed for them. We also ran a significant amount of professional development with teaching staff looking at how to differentiate for these classes, and to provide greater scaffolding when an activity was outside the classes' preferred learning style. We kept these classes in operation for several years until we removed reference to year levels all together in 2015. Many of the students from these classes looked back on these years fondly.

They expressed that the teachers really did try to teach them in a way that suited their needs, and they felt an affinity with those around them who learnt in similar ways. I maintain that we did not stream the students because we provided only a class recommendation based on their preferences and the students could ask to move groups throughout the year, which several did. At most I would agree it was 'self-selected streaming'. Perhaps most importantly, it started a welcomed conversation around meta cognition, an awareness and exploration of one's own learning preferences, among students, staff and parents.

The other bonus was that students in the Independent Accelerated Learning class were able to progress at a rate that far exceeded the average. This became a significant drawcard for the school from parents with gifted students who were bored in their existing primary as well as secondary schools. This was the class where we had a young man, Josh, twelve years of age, who asked if he could sit in the back of a Year 12 physics class. He subsequently enrolled in Year 11 physics the following year, and I spoke about his experience on my TEDx talk in 2014 – www.youtube.com/watch?v=nMxqEkg3wQ0&ab_channel=TEDxTalks

When we were constructing Josh's Year 8 timetable, his physics class fitted in better with the Year 9 program, so Josh became a Year 8, enrolled in Year 9, studying Year 11, having done Year 12 in Year 7.

PROMOTING PERSONALISED LEARNING

As an artifact of the time, I ask you to consider the tone and structure of this advertisement that ran in the local paper. There is a fine line between opening up people's minds to new opportunities and begging people to take a look. I am not sure that the balance here was right, but I think the honesty and passion for the learning community that we hoped to build together comes through.

Take Another Look!

Dear Prospective Parent,

As you know selecting the right school for your child is a very important decision.

You may have been doing your research over the last few years and may have already made your decision. But what if an exciting new option became available? What if an option that you had previously dismissed suddenly and dramatically improved?

Since being appointed as Principal in Term 4, 2009 I have worked with the leadership group and staff to achieve the following significant changes:

- Our latest innovation will be offering classes in Year 7 from 2011 which cater more closely to each student's preferred learning style. Practically this means that students will be taught in ways they like and be given additional support during activities that may come less naturally to them. How is that for personalised learning!

- A new engaging curriculum focusing heavily on improving literacy and numeracy in Years 7 to 9 as the building blocks to achieve success in the later years.

- An emphasis on personalised learning so that students have greater ownership and enjoyment in what they are studying. Many schools claim this, but at Templestowe students from Year 7 can choose 30% of their course through a range of student directed electives.

- Our students now have a head start in developing their ICT ability and can take advantage of the latest learning technologies available in all their classes. Templestowe students in Years 7 to 11 all have their own Netbook computer. We are only the third Government School in Victoria to do this!

- Our students select their own Learning Mentor as someone to assist them with school issues and help them with their learning. Because you as the parent know that your child likes this person and that they like your child and have actively committed to helping them, this reduces the reluctance parents can sometimes feel at secondary school to raising issues. No other local school offers this.

- A strong emphasis on improving VCE results, by providing increased teaching time, providing after school help classes in Sciences, English and Maths run by teachers four nights per week.

- Opening our Resource Centre from 7am to 5pm as a warm place for students to study in comfort with a Milo!

Templestowe College has changed and will continue to improve as we strive to best meet the needs of our learning community! I personally invite you to meet with me to discuss your child's education and take a tour of the school. The best way I know to decide if a school is right for your child is to visit during the day and feel "the vibe". We do not run Open Days which can often give a false impression of the school. Instead I invite you to have a real tour. Look at all classes, speak to real students you select, even look in the student toilets! Evening tours are also available by request.

Templestowe is a great school, and improving every day. Why not give me a call?

THE SUPPORTED MODEL OF CONTROL

When we first handed responsibility for planning activities and excursions over to students, some interesting things happened. Students took on opportunities with great enthusiasm and proposed a number of exciting excursions, some of which were quite sophisticated and would require a significant degree of planning. While we understood that a number of these projects would initially fail, we rationalised that that students would still learn a lot along the way, select smaller more achievable projects and improve upon their planning efforts next time. However, what we discovered was that when students did fail, they became quite despondent. There would, in reality, be no next time, and at one point I was horrified to overhear a student talking to another saying, 'Don't try it, they won't support you.' This was obviously entirely contrary to what we were trying to achieve in building student empowerment.

So from this point on, the rule among staff supporting these initiatives was that we would allow the organising student to 'smell the fear of failure', experience a sleepless night or two, but we would always provide the students with just enough support so that they were able to succeed. In some cases, this meant that we metaphorically carried the student to the finish line and threw them over. I worried whether we were being authentic when we claimed these were student-run activities, because often Assistant Principal Sally played a huge role in the organisation and running of the activity. What we discovered over time was that when a student proposed to run an activity or an excursion, we could refer them to another student who had previously organised a similar thing. To my surprise, the more experienced student could speak to this new student with a significant amount of authority and detail about how they overcame various obstacles in the planning and implementation process. When overhearing them I would think to myself, 'But YOU didn't do that bit, Sally did!' They had seemingly learnt the necessary skills from working alongside Sally and had little appreciation or understanding of how much support they had actually received. Initially I was surprised by this, but upon reflection we should realise that young people are forever receiving large amounts of assistance and scaffolding of their learning from parents and teachers and yet still genuinely feel it is their own learning. From their perspective, *they* were indeed planning and running their own excursions. Over time we saw the amount of support that we as staff needed to provide diminish, as students were able to call on each other and they were able to build upon the success of previous excursions which they had seen planned by other students. Ultimately this became known as the Supported Model of Control, where we provide just enough support to see students succeed.

'YES IS THE DEFAULT'

I am not exactly sure how I came up with this idea, but I think it was in bed one Sunday morning, working on my favourite pursuit – How were we going to turn this school around? Like many keen educators, I often spent the weekend scouring the internet searching terms like 'innovative schools' or 'school transformation' and trying to find great ideas from around the world that could be adapted to our setting. It was during one of these quests when I realised that different people want different things from their schooling experience. Some people liked more tradition, some were marks obsessed, some wanted sport, some liked things to be more flexible and 'homey.' How could the one school simultaneously meet all these needs? The answer was clear that no one whole school approach could, but it led me to think about the enormous amounts of rigidity and rules that we apply to ALL students that really only some of our families wanted.

I wondered what would be the conditions that would allow people, students, staff and parents alike to tailor-make their own schooling experience based on their own wants and needs. Could a school simultaneously support students who wanted to maximise their Australian Tertiary Admissions Rank, presumably to get into a course that required this kind of entry, while simultaneously catering for a student who was clear on their pathway into a trade or entrepreneurship who really wanted to do the bare minimum of compulsory study and couldn't give a damn about their academic results in favour of spending time pursuing their own strengths and passions. Gradually I worked through the process in my mind.

The first limitation I could envisage was time. Our staff time. Without the chores of life and responsibilities young people seem to have far more discretionary time than adults. I was happy for students, staff or parents to make modifications to their learning that took up more of *their* time, indeed many worthwhile learning pursuits are immensely time intensive. It just could not add on a lot of additional time within the allocated work hours for staff.

If you gave people a free choice to change things about their schooling program, one person's wish could not take a disproportionate amount of the school's funds. In the state system, once the costs of staff (around 80% of all costs in government schools) and then unavoidable overheads such as power, photocopying, professional development, water, cleaning etc. have been taken out, the unallocated funds in most schools amount to around $120 per student for the year. Think of that – with 200 school days, that is obviously less than a dollar per day. That is insane given that most of our students would not think to spend $10 on lunch. I realised many students were having their education seriously limited by a lack of funds. The size and quality of their projects, their travel to integrate their learning within the community, was limited to a few hundred dollars per year. It could however be subsidised by parents. As I made clear to parents on school tours, 'I want the very best of equipment and materials to support our young people's learning.' I would then quip, as I have said to the staff, 'In our troubled days, the reason people were not coming was not because we were charging too much!' which usually got a laugh.

As I would explain to parents on the tour, an idea can take as much of their money as they like, and it can even take some of ours, just not a disproportionate amount. It also depends on how great the idea or suggestion is. If it benefits lots of students in a significant way, I will find the money. It really does depend on how many students benefit and to what degree.

The final caveat was that in the school agreeing to any suggestion, that the outcome could not have any significant negative impact on someone else. One could not ask to get what *they* want while simultaneously unfairly impacting on someone else. For example, a student wanting to study a subject beyond their year level, could not do so if they lacked the basic preliminary knowledge to do so, otherwise while they might be capable of studying the material, it could potentially disadvantage the other students by taking the teacher's attention in bringing them up to speed. The solution arrived at was to give the student the end of subject test for the previous level, if they could pass they were accelerated, if not they could join as soon as they could.

These three caveats taken together became known as the 'Yes is the default' policy. 'If any student, staff member or parent has a suggestion or a request, the answer has to be "YES", unless it takes too much time, too much money or negatively impacts on someone else.'

TC's 'YES is the default' policy was recognised in 2017 by the Finnish HundrED organisation as one of the most innovative educational concepts in the world.

I am a great believer in developing a highly consistent language around school culture and it is best if it is used with some degree of precision. So 'Yes is the default', not 'The default is Yes' or 'The answer is Yes'. Likewise, the order is time, money, negative impact on others. As soon as people vary the language the power of embedding the concept is weakened. This meant not allowing ANYONE to get the order wrong, particularly publicly. I always attempted to call people out on this in a light-hearted and jovial way; while it may not always have been appreciated by them, the point was made to all who were there to be accurate in our language use around the school's vision and policies.

On a small number of occasions, the 'YES is the default' rule did bring students and parents into conflict, with the parent wanting to make a change that the student disagreed with or vice versa. In these rare cases we would willingly offer to mediate the dispute. Often heated arguments at home would be discussed most rationally around my student-made coffee table, almost always reaching a mutually agreed outcome. I would start and end these discussions with how fantastic it was that the student and their parent felt so passionately that they wanted to engage in a meaningful and rational debate and that we were part of a school that not only supported but actively encouraged this discussion. I feel like this moved the mindset from one of disagreement to a positive celebration that both participants cared deeply about the young person's education.

Our commitment to student agency

'TC acknowledges that it is the student's learning, not their parent's or that of educators, and as such it is the student who must take responsibility for their learning.'

– TC Prospectus

APPEAL ANY DECISION

All schools have rules, policies and procedures, but often how they are implemented can bear little resemblance to what the writers initially intended. Given the precarious nature of the school, I did not want even a single case of someone electing to leave the school discontented that we had not delivered what I had promised them on enrolment. One negative disgruntled voice rolling through the community can undo a lot of positive work.

We implemented an appeals system where any person, student, staff or parent who wanted to appeal directly to the principal could do so. That way, on any exit interview or conversation with a parent, I could say to anyone with a complaint, 'Unless I have said no, then you just have not gone high enough.' While the me of today abhors this hierarchical language, it was what was used at the time. When I was talking this through with students, they asked, 'But what if our complaint is about you?' A good question, so I appointed Assistant Principal Sally, as the fallback arbiter for the keeper of culture. When making a decision, schools so often side with the person highest in the hierarchy. It is almost an expectation to take the word of an adult over that of a young person. In our case, it was said to staff and students that the decision would be made on the balance of probability, given the facts. In reality very few people over the years formally appealed a decision, but I feel far better about the fact that there was a formal mechanism in place that all members of the community could rely on.

Chapter Eight

CREATING A POSITIVE
LEARNING ENVIRONMENT

SOME UNACCEPTABLE BEHAVIOUR IS INEVITABLE

Educators are on the whole compassionate, and there are many saviours among us that always want to see the best in people and give everyone another chance. This is one of the things that I really admire and enjoy about education, *yet unacceptable behaviour is a natural phenomenon when dealing with people, particularly young people.*

In schools we must accept that we will always have to graciously bear some cost of students (and staff) going through difficult times. These can be costs to the 'good order' of daily operations, to the public image of the school, even the emotional and physical safety of students and staff. To not accept this as an inevitable part of schooling is to restrict the mental model of the organisation to mere academic transmission rather than a developer of the whole child. I have never met a stand-alone brain waiting to be engaged with, an empty vessel to be filled, but always one occupying a whole child. Given the nature of humans, the developmental state of young people's brains, the VUCA (volatile, uncertain, complex and ambiguous) social constructs that we operate in, and while we should rightly take appropriate corrective action, we should NOT be surprised. Indeed, we should be delighted that there is not more of it.

You need a viable school as the first step

Unfortunately, you cannot take on too many troubled kids into a school you are trying to turn around, even if these are the very kids that will potentially benefit the most. First, you need a viable school. Too many high-needs students will flood the life raft. When this happens, you will end up with a dysfunctional school that serves no one's needs other than as a holding pen for the real world, which can actually reinforce and spread the undesirable behaviours to other vulnerable young people.

Initially I found it strange to observe young people and occasionally their parents, who were openly hostile to the school and everything we seemed to do, fight so hard to remain. On reflection, while they may not like the school, it is often the only place of consistency for the student and their family. They also usually know that while we might occasionally be in significant disagreement regarding disciplinary consequences, they did know we cared.

THE CLEAR RULES POLICY

While a number of students were certainly on board with the new directions, the way many students behaved in classes and around the school was far from ideal. I introduced a compliance system that I had previously developed and refined with significant success in two previous schools where I had been the Assistant Principal in charge of the student behaviour standards among other things. Over time I had codified the range of common misdemeanours, transgressions and more serious offences and developed a consistent set of sanctions and a method for staff to record them using observation slips that were then collated and allowed us to form an overall picture of each student's behaviour over time.

This was often appreciated by many of the students who said that it provided clear guidance and consistency as to how staff applied the school rules. Even some of the 'naughty' students said they liked it, because they were tired of 'the goodie-goodie' kids getting away with the same things they were getting in trouble for. The staff were often supportive in theory, but less so in application. Understandably, many did not like the potential for conflict when giving the student the clear rules slip, a little like a parking inspector. I had explained at a whole school assembly that it was not the staff's choice as to whether they gave out a slip and indeed the staff member would get into trouble if they didn't. In talking with staff who said that they had their own methods for dealing with incidents in class, my comment was that while they may have more effective methods, they were in effect not supporting their colleagues who did not have that level of sophistication in their student management skillset. As in previous schools, it was only once we introduced and monitored a quota system that all staff followed through and the system became a huge success in rapidly improving behaviour.

The system did provide the opportunity for staff to record positive as well as negative behaviours. I tried every measure I could think of at the time to encourage this, even suggesting that staff could only submit a negative when they had observed two positives about other students. This fell flat when staff submitted banal comments like 'was helpful' or 'worked well' which while meeting the criteria, did not achieve my aim of trying to get staff to see and reward the good in students as well as their transgressions. The reality was staff were so busy, so I fell back to focusing on the change that I really wanted, which was to track and ultimately stop the unacceptable behaviour. This was now able to be substantiated with students and their parents with specifics compiled across a range of staff, dates, and places. This system proved very effective and was difficult for students or their parents to dispute.

When 'naughty kids' like Clear Rules

When you analyse behavioural data in this way, these students' claims are often true. Those who transgress the rules often get picked up for the vast majority of the things they do, whereas those who have built up credit and good relationships with their teachers have some of the same lesser infractions ignored or they receive only a warning. I often find it is those students who come into conflict with the school's disciplinary system who have a heightened sense of fairness and perceived injustice. They were often the ones who said they liked the Clear Rules System the most, because it was clearly and consistently communicated, understood and applied.

Looking back on the Clear Rules now, I am a little embarrassed to say that I was the one who initiated this process as it gave almost no opportunity for students to develop self-discipline. There was a clear upside however in that over time, the standards of observable behaviour improved and as a consequence the amount of class time that was spent productively. The system was dropped after two years when all subjects became an elective which saw recorded disciplinary events dropped by 80%! This was quite a positive surprise. When I ran a focus group to try and understand this dramatic decrease in unacceptable behaviours, one student summed it up nicely. 'Why would you muck around, when you can study what you want, at the right level, and you have a say in what you do?'

A small number of our existing students did not like the measures we were taking to rein in their unacceptable behaviour. This is not really surprising as we were destabilising the existing power structure where a small number of the students were standing over their peers and even intimidating a number of the staff. Many disenfranchised students could not articulate their frustration, so instead expressed their outrage through graffiti. This remained an ongoing issue for the first few years of the new TC. In the end I asked staff to take a photo of 'tags' that they saw in students' books and we accumulated a graffiti library that we could then use to identify perpetrators.

Still a place for Clear Rules

Even now, ten years on, if I were moving into a school that was in trouble, where the students would not engage in respectful conversation, or where students had taken over effective control of the school, I would strongly consider something like a Clear Rules Policy... but only for a defined period. I would use a school assembly to explain the vision for the school that I, the Leadership Team and staff wanted to establish, but in order to share control with the students we would first of all need basic civil order. Thus, almost like declaring a state of emergency, for a set period I would invoke a Clear Rules Policy with a set review period to be reviewed with the SRC, in say six months. I would also seek to get their input to develop and endorse the details of the policy prior to its release.

Clear Rules for Templestowe College

	Unacceptable Behaviour	Consequence	Responsibility

1	Uniform
	a. Incorrect Uniform without a pass (Pink slip)
	  • Incorrect uniform = No excursions
	  • Where possible temporary uniform will be provided and back to class
	b. Incorrect or no sports uniform
	c. Jewellery outside uniform code
	d. Makeup outside uniform code
		Infringements per term:
		3 = Learning Mentor speaks to student and contacts parents.
		6 = Head of House speaks to student, contacts parents + Lunchtime Detention.
			All staff issue observation slips.
			Head of House Admin Assistant to record details.
			Heads of House to supervise detentions.

2	a. Late to class b. Not equipped for class c. No out of class pass d. No absence note (2 days' grace) e. Mobile phone, MP3 or technology used inappropriately f. Socially inappropriate language (mild)	9 = Head of House speaks to the student, + parent interview + Afterschool Detention. 12 = Individual program with HOH & AP	
3	Prohibited items a. Incl: permanent marker, lasers, lighters, matches *Teachers are asked not to confiscate items of significant value, but instead refer the matter to an Assistant Principal.*		

	Unacceptable Behaviour	Consequence	Responsibility
4	a. Littering in the yard or buildings b. Missing a lunchtime or classroom detention c. Spitting, spitballs d. Interfering with/defacing the work of another student e. Leaving class without permission f. Out of bounds (first offence) g. Disruption of classroom or lunchtime detention h. Interfering with the belongings of others incl locks, lockers i. Damage to college equipment incl grafitti (minor) j. Failing to return Netbook k. Installing inappropriate content on Netbook or network	Afterschool Detention + Students may be banned from the network	Head of House
	Classroom matters dealt with as part of the classroom teacher's normal disciplinary responsibility.		
5	a. Backchat/lack of manners/respect b. Failure to use class time appropriately c. Disruption of the learning environment – minor d. Misuse of College equipment e. Interfering with the belongings of others in class f. Failure to follow instructions (minor) g. Use of computer chat rooms, social network sites, playing games during class time	At the teacher's discretion • Warning (optional) • Classroom Detention • Learning Mentor consulted • Parent call by teacher • HOH informed **Sanctions as per 1 & 2**	Classroom teacher to complete slip and take detentions if appropriate. **SLIPS MUST BE COMPLETED**

	Unacceptable Behaviour	Consequence	Responsibility
6	a. Significant ongoing disruption of the learning environment b. Refusal to follow instructions (significant) c. Creating an unsafe environment (inside or outside class) d. Gross misconduct *This should be referred to the Head of House or Assistant Principal as soon as possible.*	Time Out & Parent called by teacher in consultation with the Mentor **Further sanctions may result.**	All staff TIME OUT SHEET MUST BE COMPLETED
7	Smoking or Passive Smoking (Students smell of smoke, or in the presence of smokers)	As per Smoking Policy	Head of House
8	a. Late to School (unexplained) b. Missing a class c. Truancy ie. wagging school	Afterschool Det. Internal suspension Restricted area contract	Head of House
9	Unreported damage/vandalism graffiti *Accidents do happen. All breakages must be immediately reported to the Business Manager or an Assistant Principal.*	Afterschool/Suspension Parents contacted Recovery of costs or extra duties to meet costs	Business Manager & Assistant Principal

Unacceptable Behaviour	Consequence	Responsibility
10 a. Physical violence b. Substance abuse incl. smoking repeat offenders c. Conduct prejudicial to the good order of the College d. Nonattendance/disruption of Time Out or afterschool detention e. Serious verbal abuse of another person f. Ongoing or significant failure to follow instructions g. Serious breach of Bullying Policy h. Breach of student disciplinary contract i. Creating an unsafe environment (significant) j. Computer hacking or accessing another person's files	Suspension (Internal or External) or Expulsion	Head of House, Assistant Principal, Principal

No set of rules can cover every situation and as such sanctions or procedures may be varied at the discretion of a member of the Principal Class.

The ONLY acceptable brain food/drinks for class are: fruit, muesli bars, dried fruit, water. No food to be taken into Science, ICT rooms, technology rooms for safety reasons

CREATED: AUG 2010 NEXT REVIEW: OCT 2011 Comments or suggestions to Assistant Principal Sally

DON'T SINK THE LIFE RAFT

While small schools are often inundated with students with special learning and physical needs, they are also often inundated with applications from students with significant behavioural difficulties. Certainly when I arrived at TC, we had more than a reasonable number of students with quite poor behaviour. When numbers are tight, school leaders can be tempted to hang onto every enrolment they can. Let me be clear, if your decision to retain rather than expel a student with poor behaviour is influenced by your concern about enrolment numbers, then this is a terrible decision, particularly if it involves bullying of other students. As well as being morally wrong to tolerate such behaviour, it also makes no financial sense. Inevitably, well-behaved students will leave because of the poorly behaved student and you will still be left with the instigator of the issue.

I have a genuine compassion for students with significant behavioural needs and I acknowledge that it almost inevitably stems from a series of environmental circumstances beyond the young person's control, however a struggling school as a living community can only do so much. In my view you first need to build a viable school community with a positive school culture, then once established I believe all such schools have a responsibility to take on and work with a certain percentage of youth with significant behavioural needs. The power of a positive school culture to normalise and enculturate troubled young people is immense. Such young people obviously need specialist support throughout this process, but this is far more achievable in a larger well-functioning school, with an established positive culture than in a troubled school. Even then the number and timing of taking on of new students with known behavioural difficulties needs to be carefully and consciously monitored. While the influence of the troubled student is unlikely to be enough to impact the overall positive school culture, they can turn several vulnerable students to follow them down the same self-destructive path.

SERIOUS INCIDENTS AND NON-NEGOTIABLES

I explained to students, staff and families that as the overall school leader it was my role alone to be the scales when deciding to invoke the most serious of sanctions, expulsion. The principal must weigh up the cost to the individual of severing them from the school community versus the likely costs to building and maintaining a positive school culture if they were to remain. We must accept that if this cost becomes too negative then the student must be expelled. On several occasions I had to remind teachers and senior staff to not anticipate this decision in spite of *their* perceptions of the situation, as they often did not have the full picture of the young person's external circumstances. I would explain to staff that as the principal this was my decision alone and that I wanted them to never give up on a young person and continue to focus on working with the young person as positively as possible until the student's final day. It is my regret that we did expel several students in those first few years and, in fact, throughout my time with the school. These were in many ways the toughest decisions we make as educators and I genuinely tried to continue to work with the young person and the family until they were established in their new educational or work setting, but I accept that this did not always work. This transitional support is thankfully mandated in the Victorian Government System, but at TC we would seek to meet the spirit of these provisions, not just the letter of the regulation.

In a well-functioning school there should be little recourse to suspensions and expulsions, and indeed in the final few years at TC that was the case. Our aspiration was that a student would have to actively try to sabotage their own education to fail at TC. I am sure we did not always achieve this gold standard, but that was our ambition for nurturing young people. I certainly concur with the research that both suspensions and expulsions are in fact detrimental to the student, but

I do believe that they can assist in creating a positive school culture by showing clear boundaries as to what is acceptable behaviour.

Non-negotiables – physical violence

Physical violence, particularly domestic violence, is a significant issue in our society. I believe that schools must take a strong stance to say that violence in any form is unacceptable. So, at TC any violence, even striking in self-defence resulted in an automatic suspension. There was no yelling, or intimidation on the part of staff with either the student or the family, but rather a discussion around the need to maintain a violence-free environment. We explained that it was not a permanent stain on their record and that it did not preclude them from leadership or any other activity or opportunity, but rather it was a statement to the whole community that violence in any form could not be tolerated.

Non-negotiables – bullying

Bullying is obviously another significant issue schools and work-places have to negotiate. We openly claimed to maintain a bully-free environment at TC. That is, so far as we were informed, we would continue to take action to resolve the matter until either the bullying behaviour stopped or the student(s) were expelled. Those were our guarantees to both students and parents. Our aim was to intervene earlier rather than later, ideally before the behaviour warranted disciplinary consequences, because then there is a greater likelihood of reprisals. It was a very simple but effective process. Once we had established what we believed to be the full facts we would get the parties together and explain that in a school our size it was unavoidable not to interact with each other, explained the bullying policy and said that it must stop, or someone was going to be expelled. While we looked for both parties to acknowledge any wrong-doing, apologies were never forced. So far pretty standard. We then scheduled a series of separate follow-ups to ensure that the truce was holding, the next day, two school days after that, a week after that, two weeks after that and a month after that. All these two-minute catch-ups were programmed into diaries and daily bulletins at the start of the process, and often by the end of what was now two months none of us could initially remember what we were touching base for. Sometimes the two parties had even become friends and would come up and see us together. On some occasions though, it was obvious, that in spite of assurances to the contrary, that 'something was going on' and we would recommence the investigation. Very rarely did this not resolve the situation, but on a small number of occasions a person was expelled, even for verbal bullying, where the student could or would not change their behaviour.

We were also very conscious that this bully-free environment could only be guaranteed where staff were made aware of the bullying. We endeavoured to develop a culture where students actively looked out for one another and would either deal with an issue of bullying behaviour themselves by calling it out or referring it to a staff member for support.

Our bully-free-guarantee also extended beyond the school. Even though our jurisdiction here was questionable, I would occasionally have to explain to students and parents who questioned this legitimacy, 'If we don't deal with the out-of-school stuff, it will become inside school stuff.' In dealing with online issues which became more frequent in my later years at TC, we would say to students, 'Take screen shots, DON'T respond and let us support you to deal with it.' I would publicly reiterate the promise, 'I don't want to be the leader of a community where ANY person is forced to suffer in silence and I can't guarantee that a bullying issue will be resolved the first time we intervene, but I give you my word that the bullying will stop!

Either the bully will stop or they will no longer be at the school…
provided you don't react and keep communicating with us.'

Non-negotiables – drugs

The other very serious issue that can plague schools if it becomes
part of the culture is drugs. Again, we had a well-publicised and
clear policy. Possession or consumption of cigarettes or alcohol as a
first offence resulted in a five-day suspension and parental meeting.
A second offence resulted in a five-day suspension, parental meeting and final warning that any further incident during the student's
time at the school would result in expulsion. Drug possession or
use resulted in an immediate five-day suspension, parental meeting
and final warning and information passed to police and counselling.
Any subsequent offence was automatically referred to the police and
the student was expelled. At the time a five-day suspension was the
maximum penalty that could be invoked as the Department rightly
attempted to reduce the number of days students in difficulty were
separated from the school.

Supplying or selling any drug including cigarettes resulted in an
automatic reference to police and expulsion. This sounds quite
punitive, and 'not very TC', but for me it is about protecting the
community. Possession, consumption or selling of substances is not
an accident. It requires some degree of pre-planning and secrecy in
terms of supply and consumption. Because we were so overt in regularly communicating these consequences, choosing to consume or
sell was a conscious decision that the person was putting their own
needs ahead of the collective and no longer sufficiently valued being
a part of the community.

Because we were part of the government system there were quite
strict protocols over expelling a student and on occasion the student
would have the decision turned over on appeal. The appeal process

was however quite formal and intimidating in its own right and even if they were readmitted to the school, I had made the point. As the appeal also required the parents' permission, often they also felt the best course of action was to leave. I do not like taking such a hard line with young people, but I do believe that as an institution we need to sometimes impact the individual to save the masses. It is however incumbent on the school principal to carry out these processes ethically, humanely and do their best to ensure that the student re-engages in a new setting. This is one of the hardest parts of a principal's role.

Chapter Nine

BUSINESS MATTERS

NO MONEY

We had no money to fund an extensive activities budget, and we were operating many hundreds of thousands of dollars in the red on staffing alone. We kept spending. Why?

This is where there is an important distinction between state and independent schooling, but it is partially true even there. From my days when I was briefly an insolvency accountant with Coopers and Lybrand, now PwC, I remember an institutional saying – 'If you go down (bankrupt) by a million dollars, you have a big problem. If you go down by ten million dollars, the bank's got a big problem.' The point is too many businesses go broke slowly, effectively starving to death for lack of funds. Inevitably you start dropping non-essential expenditure like painting and maintenance, and all of a sudden the place starts to look old, shabby and can give the impression of being uncared for. If your school is in a precarious financial position, you might as well go down big as go down small. I am not talking about being financially negligent. There are laws around trading while insolvent, where you continue operations and incur debts after you have a realistic inability to pay those loaned funds back. However, most people's conservatism stops them spending well short of that mark. They make financial decisions like they would as an individual, rather than as a business. If the school is not financially viable then it should close, and inevitably will, no matter what you do. But, if it still has cash reserves, then you have to play the tough game and lean into building an excellent school. That means giving an outward appearance of confidence and prosperity. People are reluctant to invest either financially or in the education of their children in an institution that has the smell of death about it and looks like it may be closed at any time.

In the case of government schools, leaders can be even more bullish. 'We work for the government' was a phrase I used often with senior management to steel their resolve when we kept spending. As an accountant, I was very conscious of our financial position but I also appreciated the materiality of the numbers. The site alone was worth an estimated $100M, so if the school did go under, the government would certainly recoup its costs. Given we had sixteen acres of prime residential land, I even enquired whether we could sell off four acres at the back of the school to give us some financial breathing space, but I was informed the proceeds of any sale would go to the Treasury, not the school or even to the Education Department, so there was no chance that we would be giving up land which we had in abundance for no net benefit.

When the Business Manager and I were eventually *invited* into the central office to discuss the school's financial position, I was quite nervous. A little like how I felt being called into the principal's office when I was a student. I had been asked to prepare a three-year forecast of student numbers, staffing and budget showing a return to profitability. With large cohorts exiting the school at the upper year levels and in spite of growth at Year 7, the overall number of students would inevitably still fall for two more years, so a return to profitability within this timeframe was simply not possible. So I took the initiative to extend out to a planned six-year time horizon showing a return to profitability in year four. When I presented the data to the Department Finance Director, Nino Napoli, he was encouraging and supportive. He took me to one side and said, 'Make sure you have plenty of fat built into those figures, because you have one shot at this and you better be able to meet those milestones!' I remember being quite surprised by this comment – it did not seem like something that finance people generally said, but I did feel like he was on our side. I was, perhaps, not quite as surprised as others when he was eventually indicted in an Independent Broad-based Anti-corruption Commission, (IBAC) enquiry, having misappropriated millions of dollars from the Education Department. Nino did make a good point, though. If you are asked to prepare figures showing that a troubled school's fortunes can be turned around, be conservative. Those in governance (the Board or School Council) and those providing the funds, be they bank or system body, like to see a school coming within budget each year on their path to returned sustainability. They do NOT like to see a leader falling short of their own financial targets, so play the figures conservatively. You will get no thanks for being financially optimistic in the planning stage.

'I didn't run this ship aground, I'm just the one trying to save it'

If you are newly appointed to leadership of a troubled school, you also have the advantage of being able to say, 'Look, I didn't get us into this position, I am just trying to get us out of it.' As leaders we often take on not only the financial burden, but the guilt associated with the school getting into the position in the first place. My stance is, if you didn't cause it, then you don't own the guilt. Just focus on making good decisions. The reality is that the school may be too far gone to turn around, but if you are too financially conservative, and not willing to spend money to improve the school, you may just ensure that you are the one on the burning deck when it does go down.

With our funding assured for the next four years, we continued to meet our milestones. It was time to bring the College Council into the picture, as they had to be comfortable with signing off on our financial strategy. Before the start of the next Board meeting, I asked them to initially meet in another space, where we shared a meal prepared by the students. After we had eaten, we returned to the boardroom where I had set up a presentation. At the time I was playing quite a bit of Texas Hold'em Poker, and I had set up a table complete with shoehorn, chips and green playing cloth down one end of the table. As I followed the Council members into the room, I said nothing, but instead let them take in the scene. There were the predictable giggles and jokes.

I took my place in the dealer's position. I explained that TC is located in a competitive market for student enrolment which they obviously knew well. I pointed to a large pile of colourful chips and said, 'This pile is East Doncaster Secondary College', who were the established market leader in the region with around 1,300 students plus an extensive waiting list. 'This pile is Doncaster Secondary College', – a slightly smaller pile of chips but still a sizeable stack. Pointing to a smaller pile, I said, 'And this is Warrandyte High School', a school of around 700 to our north. By this point people could clearly see the metaphor and laughed as we turned to the remaining stack of just six chips.

I explained that in Texas Hold'em each time the deal fell to you, you had to 'anti-up' and contribute a small stake. If you didn't choose to play a hand, eventually your stake would be eaten away slowly until you went broke. With deliberate emphasis, I said, 'When you find yourself in this position the only thing to do is wait for a good set of cards, not a great set, and go "All in." That is, put your whole stake on the line. This is where we are now. TC has to select a strategy and go "All in". We need to move quickly, change fast and we have one go at this.'

This is not a strategy where we can only make decisions at Council meetings. As the Leadership Team, we needed the freedom to make calls when needed. Because of the perilous state of the school, the parent representatives of College Council had been having a very hands-on involvement in the running of the school. This was my signal that we as a leadership group were ready to take the reins back. Given their huge commitment and contribution of time and effort over a number of years, the College Council President, Tracey, said that they were only too keen to return to a governance role and to continue to offer whatever support they could. It was a nice symbolic handing back of control to the leadership group of the school and an endorsement of my role as principal.

Hurricane Hutton Hoodie

The College Council chair gave me the nickname Hurricane Hutton, during one of our Council Meetings which was met with much laughter. While I was slightly alarmed that hurricanes are known for tearing things apart, Tracey also commented that they are almost always followed by rapid rebuilding. I had this nickname added to my school windcheater that year.

As we progressed through the next three years, enrolments at non-traditional entry points of students in Years 8-12 grew beyond our expectations to the point where we had more students joining through the middle years than we had starting with us at Year 7. It seemed that there were far more people who had already experienced secondary education, and were dissatisfied with it, than there were those wanting to take on this new model at Year 7. This unexpected growth beyond Year 7 meant that we were able to achieve a return to profitability by year three.

Alternative Revenue Streams

At TC we had another saying – 'If it's bigger than a telephone booth, we will rent it!' It seems incredibly wasteful not to utilise school facilities built with government money beyond the standard class times. In Australia even independent schools receive significant government funding towards their building programs yet most schools continue to open only 200 days per year and are used predominantly from 8.30am-4pm. With the support of Tony our Business Manager, we rented out classrooms to two Chinese schools, a Greek school, trade schools, local people offering a range of after school classes, church groups, dance classes, drama schools, holiday programs as well as the gym being booked for basketball most nights and weekends and even for parachute repacking! This amounted to thousands of dollars that we could put into the students' programs.

Many schools rent their facilities, but for a school in trouble this is doubly important as it has the potential to forge new connections to the local community and even attract new enrolments. You do have to be very careful though to ensure that the facilities and the work on display present a positive message. If your facilities are not in good condition, or the work displayed is obviously dated or of low quality, then you may be in fact be creating a negative impression. The TC foyer was usually full of parents of primary aged children collecting them from after school drama activities from 4 to 10.00pm! This was a fantastic opportunity to communicate to them about the new style of learning that we were introducing at TC. We always ensured that there were fresh brochures left on coffee tables, that the couches were clean and in good condition and the work on display was changed regularly. Likewise, we tried to provide written explanations of the process of development for the work being displayed rather than an emphasis on the finished product.

UNALLOCATED FUNDS EQUAL EDUCATIONAL OPPORTUNITIES – MAXIMISING PARENTAL PAYMENTS

At the time in Victorian government schools, you could not enforce payment for electives, but you could restrict the students' access to materials to the minimum required to learn the skills and meet the learning objectives. Government schools in less affluent areas receive extra funds because often their parents do not pay school fees. TC received no such funding and the vast majority of our parents were well off. Thus we felt quite justified in passing on the cost of materials, even expensive ones, rationalising that in comparison to the cost of private schooling of which 60% of students in the area were paying between $15-$30K, the TC option was an absolute bargain. As a government school we were very conscious of the need to ensure that no student's education was impacted by their family being under financial stress, but most certainly we followed up with vigour those families for fees that we could legitimately charge and who had the capacity to pay.

We had an exceptionally committed College Council Treasurer who was a retired accountant. Paul loved nothing more than riding his bike to school and sitting with a phone and the overdue fees list in hand and calling people for a conversation. He was charming, interested, could explain the charges and how the money was used to provide improved service to the students. On occasion he would also come across a concern or problem with the school, which was put forward by the parents as a reason for non-payment. The beauty of this was that firstly we became aware of the problem so that it could be fixed but after that, there was obviously no reason not to make good on the debt.

I would even call the families of those who had overdue accounts and after carefully establishing that there was no reason for the non-payment other than a 'philosophical objection to paying for any costs associated with a government school education' explain that their failure to pay was effectively taking that money away from the education of other students. I explained that our photocopier service contractor or the local bus company did not accept philosophy as payment. In a small number of cases I did say that if it was a genuine philosophical objection rather than an issue of money then we would be glad to accept receipt of a donation to their preferred charity in full payment, just to objectively demonstrate that money was not the issue. No parent ever took up this option.

I do understand that this stance may seem harsh, but I always felt that I was standing up for our students and those families who did pay. Almost no family has spare cash to throw around and all would most certainly like to receive services for free rather than pay for them. What I did not want to see was a culture established as exists in some government schools where those who 'work the system' do so at the expense of the funds available for the education of young people. Parents talk and there was certainly an understanding that you paid for the extras at TC and I would suggest 95% of parents really appreciated the clarity and fairness of this situation. As I would say with a laugh while conducting our school tours, 'I want the very best for our students, and I will make sure you pay your fees so that they can get it.' I would then explain that we had 98% parental payments and that I believed in the saying, 'Happy parents pay their fees. If they are not happy, then I want them to talk to me about why they are not happy and what we can do to fix it.'

Whether it is a private school or a government school, talking with parents about fees is something that makes most leaders very uncomfortable. There is no easy way around this other than to appreciate that you are having the conversation to support the education of your students. The more often you do this, the easier it becomes. You may have a business manager who fulfils this function, or some independent schools use debt recovery companies to make the issue more arm's length, stating that they are following the fee recovery policy of the Board. While this is good, being able to talk comfortably in otherwise uncomfortable conversations about money is a good life skill to develop.

Chapter Ten

THE PHOENIX RISES

GETTING THROUGH THE DIFFICULT TIMES

Those first two years were very, very difficult. While I was usually quite energetic and positive, the campus was so large and with so few students on site it could be quite depressing. As I walked around I could see many positive 'green-shoots' of change, but also saw so many things that I was unhappy with, be it the behaviour of students, their language, the way they interacted with each other, the state of the decrepit facilities, the way staff spoke to students or the litter on the ground, and the relentless battle we were facing with graffiti. Sometimes the enormity of the task ahead overwhelmed me and I periodically needed to retreat to my office on the pretence of doing paperwork. I knew I should not be around people at these times, because if the optimistic mask came off, I felt we were done for. Self-awareness and self-care during such times is critically important. I have known and observed many principals and leaders of troubled schools to take on PD or attend off-site meetings, volunteer for committees partly with a motivation of retaining their sanity by being away from their school. I understand this and encourage you not to judge it.

As a sample of the pressure, when the staff were asked to compile a SWOT analysis (strengths, weaknesses, opportunities and threats) for TC in March 2010 the following comment appeared… 'There are BIG expectations on the back of big promises that have been made. Parents could become disillusioned if things don't happen quick enough.' The pressure was immense.

I recall that I had a significant fear of what would happen if my trusted deputy Sally was ever away. We did not yet have the backup systems to manage daily organisation of covering extra classes and I certainly didn't feel that I had a sufficient handle on the school to run the place in her absence. Fortunately, Sally was incredibly resilient and healthy. I cannot recall her ever taking a day's sick leave in these early years and was never away for PD. I christened her Pollyanna. She kept me optimistic and on track whenever I faltered. She is the unsung hero of the TC revival and we will forever be in her debt.

There was a reasonable amount of self-medication going on at home through this phase. Not to the point of intoxication, but I did use alcohol to take the edge off so that I could sleep soundly. I made jokes to principal colleagues outside the school that I was claiming my alcohol bill as a tax deduction. There were night sweats and I would sometimes wake up in a panic. Because of the fragility of the workplace, I was not able to freely express myself in that setting, so I sometimes took my pent-up frustration out verbally on my family. There is no doubt they paid a cost and for that I am most sorry and regretful.

My recurring nightmare was standing at the front of the assembly and giving the closing address. 'Well, this is it… I would like to sincerely thank you all for your energy and commitment in trying to turn this school around. We gave it our best effort, but sadly it was not enough. Wherever you end up continuing your education, know that TC will forever remain a part of that journey. It has been an honour to work with you this past year. Stay safe, be strong.'

I felt the weight of the staff's livelihood and wellbeing on my shoulders, even though in reality, if the school did close they would be redeployed elsewhere. I felt the expectation of students and parents, while I had not caused the school to be in this position, I did not want to let them down and be the one to finally seal the school's fate.

Principal stress

Principal stress is a VERY real thing. Unfortunately, we still have the notion of 'the hero leader' who is in some ways superhuman and not impacted in the same way other adults are. This is wrong. We are just as fragile as the next person and often end up taking on the additional weight of the burdens of others. We are rarely trained or adequately prepared for the enormity of the role. Even the term Principal or Head reinforces the stereotype. As a profession, school leaders need to embrace our fragility, our fallibility and share the load. If we want to attract the best people who stay healthy so that they can make high-quality decisions and form positive relationships, then the workload needs to be sustainable and the expectations of society moderated. Perhaps we all need a little addendum to our name tag and name plate on our office door.

– Peter Hutton
Principal and Human Being

DID THAT MOVE?

For the first two years I wondered if any progress was being made. We would pick up a few enrolments including some students who together with their parents were signing on for the right reasons, then just as we were rejoicing, celebrating the small wins, we would hear that one of our highly involved students was going to a select entry high school or worse still, a local competitor. A student going to a neighbouring state school was always worse as inevitably they would, during the process, entice others to join them. It really felt like a battle – would we die before we could rebuild?

We were fortunate to pick up a few enrolments whose parents were quite senior in the Education Department and others whose parents were tertiary educators who could see what we were trying to achieve. On those early enrolment tours, I used this fact to emphasise that we had a disproportionate number of students whose parents were educators in order to give confidence to parents who were a little unsure if they were doing the right thing, enrolling in a school with such a different philosophy.

I used to imagine turning the school around like some herculean feat of moving a giant boulder embedded on the side of a hill. If only I could get it moving, I felt the momentum would do the rest. Metaphorically I imagined us all as a staff pushing, kicking, pressing on the boulder to move. I explained my metaphor to the staff and said that if we were all working on the same side of the boulder and pushed in unison, we would have a greater chance of success.

Each day I imagined another strategy to move the boulder, discarding what did not work and adding a few new enticements for existing students to stay and new ones to enrol. The pressure to grow the school before it shrank was immense. Two steps forward, and often two steps back. Then one day it moved. It was almost imperceptible. I can't even recall what it was. Perhaps a few more positive comments than usual on a tour. A shift in the balance between students coming for the opportunities compared to those coming for a 'fresh start' but I definitely felt the swing of momentum in a positive direction. I checked with other staff, 'Do you feel like this is moving?' Some said yes, others no. Then over the next few months, more and more positive signs started to emerge.

The confirmation finally came when our indicative numbers for our third year were released... seventy-five Year 7 students, up from fifty-four in our second year. I actually danced down the hallway and shared the news with each person, staff or student that I saw....it was working. We were going to make it!

Double down on initial positive movement

When you do sense the boulder move, it is certainly time for celebration but it is also the time to double down on your efforts. Once you have overcome inertia of getting the troubled school to move in your desired direction, now is the time to lean in and build as much initial momentum as possible. Now is the time to get even more of those positive stories of student success into the media, newsletter and onto the website. Once you have that swirl, people will want to become a part of the new story. Just like certain people thrive in a challenging and 'up against it' environment, far more people like being part of a success or turn-around story.

ADVICE TO LEADERS FOR TURNING AROUND A TROUBLED SCHOOL

Let us acknowledge that all circumstances are different, but there are some general words of advice that I think make success more likely:

- Lock out regular time for exploring innovation and growth strategies each week, no matter how busy you are. It is no use saying you will undertake this thinking and research once 'things settle down'. They won't and at best you will be left with a functioning school that looks nothing like your intended vision.

- Nurture the 'green shoots' of change. Any behaviour that looks like or supports your aspirational culture, reward it with your time and attention. In a troubled school it is easy to focus on what is wrong, but people need to see that there are aspects of their existing practices that you value and that you are enthusiastic in your affirmations.

- Write and speak publicly about your theories, ideas and ideals. Share and test them with your community and more broadly. Great ideas need to be tested and they are little use if they remain in your head.

- Reach out to well-known thought leaders now and regularly. Be audacious. Go BIG. Tell them what your plans are, invite them to visit. Ask them for a quote you can use about what they see.

- If you don't already have one, form a professional support network with people you are philosophically aligned with outside the school. Certainly, the Future Schools Alliance was created for just this purpose. You will need confidants to share this journey with. https://futureschools.education/

LEARN TO DANCE IN THE GREY

I attribute my comfort with being willing to challenge the status quo and in particular to find the grey space with interpreting rules and regulations to two disparate factors – dyslexia and my brief time in the law faculty.

There are as many types of dyslexia as there are dyslexics as it really is a blanket term thrown over all neurodivergent people that have difficulty with reading and spelling, but difficulties often flow on to writing and a range of other manifestations. My daughter Jemima, for instance, while being admitted to study medicine, cannot fathom the direction when people point at something. She obviously knows what pointing is and is intended to convey but cannot shift her 'mind's eye' to take on the perspective of the person doing the pointing.

From the time dyslexics realise that they are 'different' from their peers, the stigma and shame starts to settle in. Our society places such a high value on being able to read well that the psychological impacts on those who find that this process does not come naturally can be profound. Many dyslexics go on to develop sophisticated avoidance, distraction, masking and manipulative strategies to avoid detection and to cope in a literacy-ladened world. Many learn that the rules of school are simply not made for us, and that if we don't flex them, ignore them or break them we are pretty much guaranteed to lose that game. This is what allows us to cross the line with little hesitation or remorse.

The second element in my favour was my partially completed law degree, studied at Monash University, where I gained enough knowledge to understand the law but not so much as to be accountable for my opinions! Legal process taught me to see that there was always an opposing argument and all you had to do was to keep searching until you found one. This approach served us well on many occasions as we sought to bend an inflexible system to accept an interpretation that would benefit our students.

Sidebar – Don't ask for permission

An important lesson I learnt early on was never ask for permission or clarification, but instead 'do' and beg for forgiveness. Asking for permission is almost a sure way to have your innovative idea knocked back. There is literally nothing positive for the bureaucrat in approving anything that is remotely risky, but there is potentially lots for them to lose. Many supportive bureaucrats would prefer to have the option to tactically ignore or pretend not to know of your act or omission, and then only if the plan goes wrong, to be able to lightly castigate you rather than have to shut your idea down at inception.

Most regulations are written in such a way as to govern the existing school paradigm. Rarely do they contain prohibitions for innovation as the writers could never envisage schooling occurring any other way.

Are you someone who feels compelled to ask for permission?

Could you interpret the regulations you feel are binding, more flexibly?

Do the regulations explicitly forbid you from doing what you want to do or do they have the heading 'guidelines'?

Is your mindset around 'rules' holding back your innovation journey?

The Phoenix Rising – TC Year Book Front Cover

THE PHOENIX

It was perhaps an omen that the school magazine was and still is called *The Phoenix*, that mythical bird of beauty and power recognised by many ancient civilisations that every five hundred years would hurtle to the ground, burst into flames and arise renewed. I loved the imagery of the phoenix and hopefully the parallel journey TC would take. I so wanted us to be the phoenix and not a smouldering feather duster.

At the end of my first two years, rather than delivering the 'we didn't make it, the school is closing' speech which I had rehearsed so many times in the dark hours of the morning, I chose to speak about the phoenix at our final year assembly and in the school magazine.

Principal's yearbook article – Phoenix rising

We started this year with the motto, 'Let's see what we can achieve when we work together.' Now, looking back on the year I think it is fair to say that we have made great progress to achieve our vision to be a dynamic and caring learning community, recognised for future focused personalised learning. This magazine will showcase many of the amazing events and achievements of our students. I hope it is something that members of our community will treasure and look back on in years to come. What is more difficult to capture in pictures and words is the depth of spirit which has developed at TC.

This year I have seen students take responsibility for their own learning and their lives. Students have increasingly taken up the challenge to 'drive the bus' rather than being passive learners led on an educational tour by their teachers. Students have taken a greater role in the leadership of the school, now having five representatives on the School Leadership Group which formerly comprised only the Principals and Leading Teachers. When appointing new staff, applicants are now also interviewed by a trained panel of students to assess how the person will fit within our special TC culture.

But what makes TC special is the attitude of respect and acceptance that we have for one another. As a result of the House system, vertical electives and extensive extracurricular program, divisions and tensions based on the artificial barrier of year levels has been shattered. I am extremely proud to see our older students mentor and guide our younger students, not just on special occasions but in the everyday interactions of school life.

"The Phoenix" is a great symbol for our school. TC has risen from the ashes and is becoming something truly magnificent. The Phoenix appears in the mythology and folk law of a large number of our students' backgrounds including the Greeks, Romans, Indians, Egyptians, Persians, Chinese, Japanese, Korean and Russians dating back to around 500BC. The legend goes that in a cycle lasting 500 years the Phoenix will build a nest out of twigs and wood and then when the time is right, ignite into fiercely burning flames and burn to ashes. From these ashes a magnificent new bird of red and golden feathers with a beautiful song rises. The Phoenix reminds us that sometimes we need to put an end to the past and free ourselves from our baggage, preconceptions and compromises that we have made and see the world with new eyes.

In some ways we are still the young fledgling, growing and exploring the possibilities of the future of education. We are pioneers in building a school community that it is fun to be a member of and yet also highly successful in assisting students to become ethical, confident and motivated learners. Like the phoenix we have a captivating message and we are keen to share this message about what education can be like with the world.

Phoenix

Day by day, watching bits slip, disappear
Hoping that you all will stand beside me
On my own, swimming against the tide
Trying to arrest the fears and doubts I see.

Then you'll rise before my eyes
On wings that seem to fill the sky
Like a phoenix rising, determined to fly.

Wings on fire, there are parts that burn
Out of the ashes, who ARE they?
No time to stop, like a hurricane
Into the smoke and flame, we'll fly away.

And we'll rise right before their eyes
On wings that seem to fill the sky
A phoenix rising, ready to fly.

The heart that stops with every loss
Education for all, a time and place
A vision for progress, defying the odds
The survival of the innovation case.

And we rose right before their eyes
On wings that soared and filled the sky
The phoenix risen, ascending high.

– Fiona Hutton

A CLOSE TO TC'S SURVIVAL STORY

I thank you for taking the time to read this story of our early years at TC and hope it has emboldened and offered guidance to anyone in the challenging position of turning around a troubled school. To follow the analogy I used in the introduction – it was a terribly protracted birth, interrupted by COVID, and let's face it, if you can't finish writing a book during 263 days of lockdown, when will you?

And so we draw the survival stage of the TC story to a close. We had made progress, had a few minor scars, but we now knew we would survive to fight on. We'd had almost no interaction with or interference from the Regional or Central Office at this stage, as no bureaucrat wanted to be caught in the shockwave as TC imploded. We were a spore that had accidentally blown in through an open window and landed on an agar plate of possibility. What would germinate? Could this strange growth end up being a hitherto unknown cure for something? Perhaps a sick and ailing education system?

Yours, faithfully committed to evolving new paradigms of schooling that liberate human potential and positively impact the world,

Peter Hutton

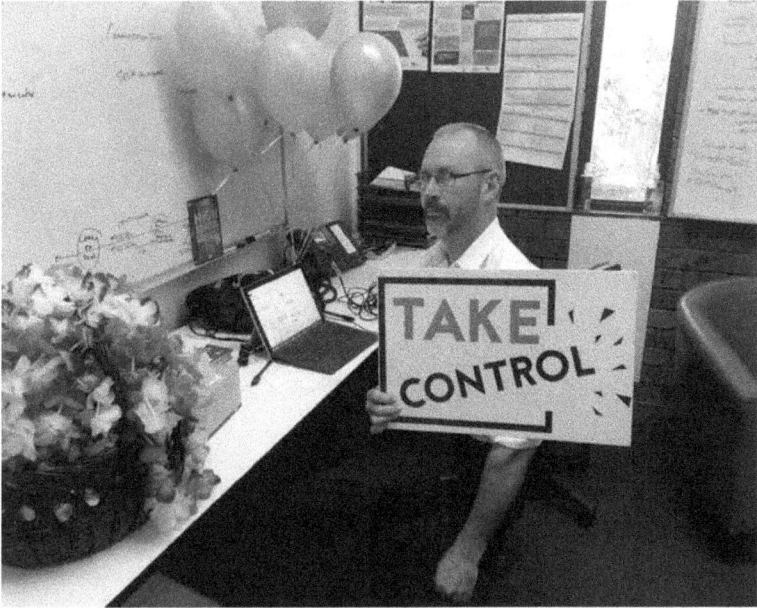

My final day at TC, in our communal office